GRAND STRATEGY FOR THE 1980s

GRAND STRATEGY FOR THE 1980s

Bruce K. Holloway
Theodore R. Milton
Bruce Palmer, Jr.
Maxwell D. Taylor
Elmo R. Zumwalt, Jr.

Edited by Bruce Palmer, Jr.

American Enterprise Institute for Public Policy Research
Washington, D.C.

ISBN 0-8447-3294-X

AEI Studies 192

Library of Congress Catalog Card No. 78-57065

Printed in the United States of America

THE AEI PUBLIC POLICY PROJECT ON NATIONAL DEFENSE

The American Enterprise Institute, as part of its foreign policy and related defense policy study program, decided in 1976 to establish a defense project in order to focus public debate on the array of vital defense issues. The project sponsors research into strategy, threat, force structure, defense economics, civil-military relations, and other areas— and presents the results in publications such as this one and the unique *AEI Defense Review* series. In addition it sponsors forums, debates, and conferences, some of which are televised nationally.

The project is chaired by Melvin R. Laird, former congressman, secretary of defense, domestic counsellor to the President, and now senior counsellor of *Reader's Digest*. The twenty-four member advisory council represents a broad range of defense viewpoints. The project director is Robert J. Pranger, head of AEI's foreign and defense policy studies program. General Bruce Palmer, Jr., U.S. Army (retired) serves as consultant to the chairman.

CONTENTS

FOREWORD

General Bruce Palmer, Jr., the editor of this volume, was formerly vice chief of staff of the U.S. Army and one of the army's most distinguished senior officers. In 1976, when he and I discussed the formation of the American Enterprise Institute Public Policy Project on National Defense (where he now serves as consultant to the chairman, Melvin R. Laird), we agreed on one pressing need—that more attention be given to grand strategic aspects of American global objectives and the relation of these objectives to our military power. In the history of thinking on the "art of war," the strategic dimension has been considered essential to an understanding of the role of defense and warfare in national policy. The writings of Clausewitz and Mahan immediately come to mind.

In recent years the realm of long-term strategic objectives has been dominated by civilians, rather than by persons with extensive military experience. War may be too important to be left only to the generals, but military considerations must be linked to political ones in our national strategy. In defense, perhaps strategy is too important to be left solely to those without experience in the use of military force, as a deterrent and in real armed conflict, in pursuit of political objectives. For example, it is not enough for leaders merely to assert that military power still has influence in today's world, if the conditions under which this holds true are not specified. Similarly, to argue that there exist limitations on military power does not necessarily produce any clear idea under which circumstances this is so.

Recognizing the importance of strategy for military preparedness and the significance of real mililtary power in the pursuit of strategic objectives, General Palmer has prepared this volume in collaboration with four very experienced senior officers. This volume represents the writing of national strategy from the standpoint of experience at the highest levels of command, where political and military considerations intersect. It is meant to contribute to the current strategic debate within the tradition of those with military backgrounds who have turned their thinking to the essential interactions between national purposes in international relations and the contribution of military power to such purposes.

ROBERT J. PRANGER
Director of Foreign and
Defense Policy Studies

INTRODUCTION

Bruce Palmer, Jr.

The protracted nature of the war in Vietnam ushered in a debate over the future role of the United States in world affairs. This debate, which continues today, started well before the end of U.S. involvement in Southeast Asia when, in early 1969, the administration articulated a strategy of "realistic deterrence." This new national security policy sought to redefine U.S. interests, recognize realistic limits of American military power, and spell out how the United States would meet its defense commitments throughout the world. Fundamentally, the intention was to maximize the "total force" combination of U.S. and allied military power and indicate to our allies that they must look to their own capabilities for regional defense. Integral to these efforts to bring our international commitments into line with our defense capabilities were major diplomatic initiatives moving towards détente with the Soviet Union and the People's Republic of China.

President Ford maintained the general thrust of American foreign policy and its supporting defense posture, while the country continued to debate the future U.S. role. In fact, this was a major issue in the 1976 presidential campaign and election. Since his inauguration, President Carter has undertaken a major national security review and has taken a series of initiatives in the field of foreign and defense policy. As a result, certain aspects of his approach to international affairs are beginning to emerge. So far, his policy changes seem to be a matter of emphasis, giving more attention than his predecessors to Third World affairs, while seeking to strengthen U.S. relationships with major allies, Western Europe and Japan, and downplaying U.S. relations with the Soviet Union. As yet no clear thrust or direction to the administration's foreign policy is discernible, however; rather one perceives a policy of general accommodation to a complex world and a hope for opportunities to shape a more cooperative global framework of international relations.

In the spring of 1977, the American Enterprise Institute, in developing the focus of its public policy project on national defense, consulted numerous former senior civilian and military officials of the U.S. government who had been associated with foreign affairs and defense policy. One of the themes that recurred most often in their comments was the apparent lack of a cohesive national strategy or security policy in the aftermath of the Vietnam War; several retired senior military officers, in particular, stressed this point. From there it was a short step to asking some of these men to articulate their thoughts on the subject of what might be called "grand strategy" for the United States over the next decade.

The contributors to this volume include retired four-star generals and admirals who have served in such positions as chairman of the Joint Chiefs of Staff, chief or vice chief of their service, or unified commander. All told, they represent a substantial reservoir of experience, talent, and thought. Each was asked to develop a broad concept of global strategy for the United States over the next decade, addressing the most significant nonmilitary factors as well as the purely military ones. It was suggested that, within whatever strategic nuclear forces concept the author adopted, the primary focus be on conventional, nonnuclear forces. Naturally, each contributor was expected to draw on his own particular background, experience, and expertise.

The American Enterprise Institute has recently published two other collections that are directly related to this volume. The first, *Détente and Defense*, edited by Robert J. Pranger, concerns pertinent foreign policy statements of American and Soviet officials, official documents, and articles by knowledgeable individuals on the subjects of détente and U.S. defense, with specific reference to the SALT I agreements. The second, *Nuclear Strategy and National Security: Points of View*, edited by Pranger and Roger P. Labrie, focuses on U.S. and Soviet doctrine concerning the role of strategic nuclear forces, theater nuclear warfare doctrine for NATO, American and Soviet nuclear planning, and nuclear arms control efforts since SALT I. This third collection extends the discussion by addressing U.S. national strategy for the 1980s.

1
NATIONAL POLICY TOO LIGHTLY ARMED

Maxwell D. Taylor

Diplomacy without arms is music without instruments
—Frederick the Great

History abounds in examples of states that have come to grief pursuing political goals too ambitious for the military means available for their support. In 1812, Napoleon sacrificed the Grande Armée and lost his empire in a vain effort to force Czar Alexander to conform to a continental blockade of British imports. In World War II, Hitler made a similar mistake in attacking the Soviet Union with insufficient military strength to attain his goal of Nazi hegemony from the Atlantic to the Volga. Japanese leaders of the same era had visions of conquering a vast empire rich in natural resources embracing most of eastern Asia and western Oceania, but their aspirations too exceeded their means.

While the American record contains no comparable disasters, our escape cannot be credited to exceptional wisdom or foresight. As Army Chief of Staff in the period 1955–1959, I was constantly concerned about the extent of our political commitments—most of them based on the Truman Doctrine—implying some kind of military obligation. On my office wall I kept a chart showing the forty-odd nations to which we had in effect given promissory notes backed by inadequate military assets. Today these commitments remain essentially unchanged on our national debit ledger.

In fact, since the 1950s the gap between the hopes, aspirations, and expectations of American policy and the realities of military power has constantly widened. Whereas the old commitments remain, others have been added. We have broadened our political goals and have undertaken the protection of new interests and assets at a time when adversaries and opposition have been increasing in numbers and strength. As a result, our national policy has become too lightly armed for security or success in the turbulent world which awaits us in the coming decade. This is the thesis which I hope to demonstrate.

Unfortunately for those concerned with its military support, national policy resembles the British constitution in that it is never set down in a single document but must be inferred at any given moment from a congeries of presidential statements, campaign promises, congressional pronouncements and executive agreements—any one of which is susceptible to revision or revocation on short notice. As a result, the planners in the Pentagon have constantly complained of inadequate political guidance for the design of a military establishment consistent with the needs of future policy. In its absence, they are left to their own devices, as I am in the present instance, to foresee the political trends that will affect the future tasks of the armed forces.

The Military Tasks Ahead

Since the Soviet Union is likely to remain our prime rival for world leadership, it is reasonable to expect our relations with that country to serve as a main source of tasks for our armed forces. If we are to continue to enjoy a world balance of power at least as favorable as at present, we shall wish to restrain any significant expansion of Soviet influence which might destabilize the situation in Western Europe, reopen the conflict in the Middle East, undermine our relations with key allies and trade partners, or otherwise disrupt a relatively satisfactory status quo. Such defensive objectives on our part would at a minimum require our armed forces to retain deployments about as at present in Europe, the Mediterranean, and the Western Pacific and to reexamine closely the ability of our naval forces to control essential sea lanes to and from these regions.

Our policy toward Israel will continue to place demands on our armed forces. At a minimum, we must continue to supply U.S. military equipment to Israel at past levels. In the end, we may feel obliged to give some military guarantees of protection to Israel as a price for its concessions to the Arabs in reaching a definitive peace settlement. If this is the case, we shall have added an important new entry to our list in the national commitment ledger. In any event, we must continue to maintain forces in the Mediterranean as a sign of firmness of purpose and as a brake on Soviet interventionist impulses.

Africa holds almost unlimited possibilities for trouble. While we would perhaps like to ignore most of this vast continent as being too backward or too remote to be of serious interest to the United States, recent events have reminded us of the difficulty of holding aloof from any part of the world where the Soviet Union shows an inclination to advance its influence. The fall of Angola to insurgents aided by Cuban forces and the more recent Soviet/Cuban activities in Ethiopia have sounded a warning to Washington of what to expect in Africa if we stand aside. Our awareness of the complexities of African problems is accompanied by a growing appreciation of the future economic importance of the natural resources of the region. While the situation is far too fluid to permit a forecast of possible future tasks for American forces, we can be sure that frequent crises will arise with little warning.

This mention of our interest in African resources calls attention to a most important new factor contributing to the inadequacy of our military power—a growing national dependence on imports. As a consequence of population growth, our inordinate per capita consumption of industrial products, and the consequent depletion of our natural resources, the continuation of the traditional American way of life will henceforth depend upon an endless stream of imports of raw materials, mostly from Third World countries. Already we are importing about half of our oil and meeting most of our needs for such primary minerals as chrome, bauxite, manganese, nickel, tin, and zinc. Henceforth if we are to operate an economy that can maintain our high living standards, support the armed forces, assist our allies, and give help to impoverished and hungry nations of the Third World, we must turn increasingly to foreign markets for raw materials and pay the price to assure an uninterrupted supply.

In estimating our future needs, we shall find that the foreign markets in which we are most interested are located in four regions—the Western Hemisphere as far south as about the Tropic of Capricorn, the oil fields of the Middle East, parts of Africa south of the Sahara, and the Southwest Pacific area. Within these regions we shall wish to secure oil in quantity from Canada, Venezuela, Saudi Arabia, Iran, Nigeria, and Indonesia, but we must be always on the lookout for new sources elsewhere. In the case of minerals, we can find in the Western Hemisphere important quantities of those in greatest demand, but we shall need redundant or alternate sources in countries such as Australia, Malaysia, Zaire, Zambia, and South Africa. It would simplify the tasks of our Navy, which is responsible for protecting the commercial sea routes, if we could limit our trade with Middle Eastern and Mediterranean markets since they are likely to become inaccessible in time of war. Equally, the Department of State would be happy to forgo close trade partnerships with Rhodesia and South Africa out of concern for relations with black African states.

Our need for a continuous input of raw materials from abroad gives new meaning to our diplomatic relations with the Third World. Unhappily, we must anticipate difficulties in our dealings with many countries of this group because of our seeming neglect of them in the past and their newly developed bloc consciousness. Although the nations with which we shall be most interested in establishing long-term economic relations are not among the most impoverished, most of them can be expected to join in support of the common cause which unites have-nots in resentment against the western industrialists and particularly against the United States, a symbol of wasteful affluence. Their discontent with the economic status quo has led to demands for a progressive transfer of wealth from rich to poor nations and the eventual establishment of a new economic order free of inequities. Although industrial nations in their present complacency pay little heed to such revolutionary vaporings, the fact remains that a North-South confrontation promises to replace or at least to accompany that of East versus West, which since World War II has constituted the primary threat to world peace. In any case, the international political climate is likely to prove an obstacle to American commercial relations in many of the regions of the Third World containing the raw materials we shall require.

Even if our diplomats eventually succeed in overcoming the anti-American bias and in establishing firm relations with selected producer countries, our foreign trade will henceforth be exposed to dangers and uncertainties. Many contingencies may arise to obstruct the vital continuity of imports—overt acts of war or covert peacetime acts of terrorism taking such forms as sabotage of shipping, piracy, clandestine minelaying, or guerrilla sea warfare. The mere report, true or false, of an unidentified submarine in the straits of Malacca or Hormuz could interrupt all tanker traffic to western ports for a considerable time. In the light of the recent history of international terrorism, these can hardly be dismissed as fanciful conjectures.

Less dramatic dangers to our commerce could stem from acts of economic warfare—price-jacking by producer countries or the formation of OPEC-like cartels in scarce materials such as bauxite, tin, or manganese. There is always a possibility of embargoes by exporters wishing to moderate the rate of depletion of their limited national reserves. Trade could be interrupted by political disturbances in supplier countries resulting from internal instability or from external incitement. To all such disruptions, the Soviet Union could be expected to lend a willing and practiced hand. Over time, such obstacles to trade could produce serious fluctuations in the output of the American economy that would injure the national prosperity and impair our ability to conduct and sustain military operations.

The Inadequacy of Our Armed Forces

As I survey this long list of old and new tasks and the conditions under which the armed forces may be expected to perform them, I am deeply impressed by the present inadequacy of our military forces. There are a number of grounds for my pessimism. To begin with, despite political oratory to the effect that the United States is and must always remain second to none in military strength, the fact is that our forces have fallen behind those of the Soviet Union in many categories, and their capabilities are not commensurate with the tasks they are likely to be called upon to perform.

The growth of the Soviet navy creates justified concern among security planners in Washington. In the course of the current expansion of the Soviet military establishment, the Soviet navy has become numerically superior to our fleet in both surface combat ships and sea-going submarines, the latter by nearly three to one. It is a navy clearly designed to challenge American control of important sea areas and to give the Soviet Union a capability for military intervention overseas at a distance from its frontiers. The impression of American leaders regarding the wartime capabilities of the Soviet submarine fleet, which now includes some 250 boats, was clearly expressed by Secretary of Defense Rumsfeld in his budget report for FY 1977:

> The current [U.S.] fleet can control the North Atlantic sea lanes to Europe but only after serious losses to United States and allied shipping and our ability to operate in the Eastern Mediterranean would be, at best, uncertain. The fleet in the Pacific could hold open the sea lanes to Hawaii and Alaska but, because of a shortage of surface combatants, would have difficulty in protecting our lines of communication into the Western Pacific. This situation will presumably grow more precarious as the capabilities of Soviet nuclear attack submarines increase.[1]

In short, it was the view of the Secretary of Defense that, in a major war involving the Soviet Union, we would have great difficulty supporting NATO in case of an attack and reinforcing our forces in Europe. In the face of Soviet opposition, our Navy could not count on operating in the eastern Mediterranean in support of Israel or in the Western Pacific in support of Japan and Korea. The Secretary further warned that this situation will become more difficult if the Soviet nuclear submarine fleet continues to increase as expected.

[1] Annual Defense Department Report FY 1977, p. v.

In the years ahead, the freedom of action of our forces overseas will be restricted not only by the Soviet submarine force but also by a shortage of secure bases needed to provide logistic support for distant operations. In the Mediterranean, which until recently was a NATO lake, political instability in Portugal, Italy, and Spain along with anti-American feeling in both Greece and Turkey now renders uncertain our access to the ports and airfields which would be essential in the conduct of military operations. Judging by the attitude of our NATO allies toward the transfer of American military equipment from Europe to Israel after the 1973 war, we can look for no assistance from them outside the geographic boundaries of the alliance.

In the Persian Gulf region, we have never had a military base worthy of the name, and the same can be said for all of Africa south of the Sahara. Although we still have bases in Northeast Asia, we have announced an intention to make a progressive reduction of our ground forces in Korea. In the resource-rich areas of Southeast Asia and the Southwest Pacific, we have no foothold of importance except in the Philippines, where President Marcos recurrently expresses dissatisfaction over our presence. Thus a combination of increased Soviet submarine strength and a shortage of properly situated bases threatens to clip the strategic wings of our armed forces and thereby shorten their effective reach.

In an ideal world, we would have potent allies with strength capable of offsetting some of our deficiencies, but such is not the case. We have already noted the instability of the southern flank of NATO from Portugal to Turkey. While the conditions in allied countries north of the Alps are not so serious, many governments are fragile, subsisting on paper-thin parliamentary majorities and preoccupied with economic slowdowns, the rising price of oil, and the growth of local Communist parties. Such debilities, accompanied by prolonged apathy toward the improvement of national military establishments, discourage any reasonable hope that, in case of a major attack, the alliance could conduct a protracted defense of Western Europe even with substantial American reinforcements.

In the Far East, Japan is suffering from essentially the same economic ills as Europe. It is wholly dependent on imported oil, most of it tankered over a long, unprotected supply line from fields in the Middle East across the Indian Ocean and through the Malacca Straits. With only a small navy for local defense, the nation is vulnerable to the slightest interruption of this lifeline.

Certain impediments to the effectiveness of our armed forces are largely of our own creation. In contrast to the Soviet Union, which has built up its armed forces rapidly, in recent years we have permitted our own to decline steadily in trained manpower, aircraft, ships, submarines, and reserves of war equipment. This decline has been in large part the result of repeated reductions in the military budget both in purchasing power and as a percentage of the gross national product.

Over the same period, primarily for domestic political reasons, the United States adopted an all-volunteer system of recruiting which thus far has produced volunteers adequate in number and quality to meet the peacetime needs of the active forces but inadequate in the case of the reserve forces. This latter deficiency is critical since the active forces, particularly the Army, cannot fulfill their present wartime missions without large numbers of reserve units and individual fillers ready to accompany them into combat. The fact is that, despite the high price being paid to attract and retain volunteer manpower in peace, the nation could not sustain significant forces in combat without a prompt reversion to some form of conscription. Casualty lists from overseas produce a dampening effect on youthful enthusiasm for military service, particularly in the Army.

This doubt as to the availability of adequate trained manpower in war is but one factor which creates uncertainty about our national readiness to use military force promptly and effectively. The post-Vietnam attitude of Congress and of much of the public has been one of opposition to further military intervention abroad and of distrust of limited war as an appropriate means to advance foreign policy. This antimilitary reaction, which coincided with the determination of Congress to deprive the President of his ability to involve the country in another Vietnam, produced the War Powers Act of 1973. Regardless of the merit of its purpose, the provisions of the act offer endless possibilities for prolonged debate in the time of crisis between Congress and the White House over the justification for sending troops overseas into potential combat situations and could thus constitute a formidable legal obstacle to any timely use of military force.

Although at present there are indications of change in the national mood and of some recovery of self-confidence and national pride, our past performance remains a matter of record, one which will continue to cause uncertainty abroad about our will to take sides vigorously in causes which may entail military involvements. Some foreign observers seriously question whether we would again resort to arms unless directly attacked ourselves, and many wonder audibly whether the President remains truly the commander in chief and prime architect of national policy. Such uncertainties weaken the credibility of the armed forces as a reliable weapon-in-being capable of deterring or suppressing armed violence promptly on presidential order.

Some Likely Contingencies

The existence of these open questions regarding the ability of the armed forces to perform the tasks necessary to support national policy invites a consideration of a few of the likely contingencies that might test their performance. The one most frequently discussed is their ability to continue to deter nuclear war, given the substantial increase in Soviet strategic weaponry.

Deterrence of Nuclear War. On this score, I would have no great concern provided we make no imprudent, unrequited concessions in the pending SALT negotiations which would result in a strategic force patently inferior to that of the Soviet Union by any acceptable measure of relative strength. Personally, I would consider adequate the deterrent capability of a U.S. force that could inflict such damage as to paralyze the Soviet government, economy, and war-making capability for an indefinite period regardless of all enemy efforts to prevent it. While the exact level of damage required to satisfy this formula is subject to wide differences of judgment, I conceive of it as at least comparable to the total losses, human and material, suffered by the Soviet Union in the course of World War II—a level which I believe our forces could impose now and which they should remain able to impose in the future.

Many will object to my regarding as adequate a deterrent force that can do no more than match the destruction caused in Russia by the German armies in World War II. In the end, did not the Soviet Union survive those losses, overcome the enemy, and end the war a victorious world leader? But in a strategic nuclear war today, the 20 million Soviet fatalities reportedly suffered in four years of conventional war would be compressed into four hours or four days at most, with a paralyzing effect on all governmental, economic, and military activities incomparably greater than that caused by the losses in World War II. There is reason to believe that, despite their extensive plans for civil defense, Soviet leaders are well aware of the irrelevance of comparisons between losses in World War II and those to be expected in unlimited strategic war. They probably share Khrushchev's recognition of the futility of civil defense when, "in a single thermonuclear flash, a bunker can be turned into a burial vault for the civilian leaders and military commanders [of a nation]."[2]

There are other reasons for confidence in the deterrent capability

[2] Nikita Khrushchev, *Khrushchev Remembers: The Last Testament* (Boston: Little, Brown & Co., 1974), p. 542.

of strategic forces such as ours. The Soviet leaders have ample cause to fear the reaction of hostile neighbors to the devastation and paralysis of the Soviet Union in the aftermath of a strategic exchange. The Chinese, Poles, Hungarians, and suppressed minorities of the Soviet Union would hardly forgo such an opportunity to settle old scores. Indeed, the surviving Russians themselves would not feel kindly toward the leaders responsible for their plight.

As a final point, let us not forget that an individual or a state may be deterred from pursuing a course of action for other reasons than fear of its consequences. There may be a safer or cheaper way to accomplish the same purpose at lesser cost or risk. Thus, one would expect that the Soviet leaders, in their determination to destroy their archrival and thereby to hasten the advent of global communism, would recognize the advantages of relying on time and on the inherent weaknesses of the capitalist system to bring down the United States and its associates. In the meantime, they could exploit their strategic armaments with comparative safety to intimidate faint-hearted opponents and neutrals and thus attract outriders to the communist bandwagon.

Defense of NATO. A second military contingency for which our forces must be prepared is a massive conventional attack on NATO by the Warsaw Pact. In compliance with the terms of the North Atlantic Treaty, it has been American policy for almost thirty years to contribute a force to the common defense of the alliance, one which at present amounts to some five divisions and supporting air units in Western Europe, totalling around 300,000 soldiers and airmen and almost as many dependents. In conjunction with Allied forces, their mission is to defend the German frontier against a major attack, if possible without resorting to nuclear weapons.

While this was a reasonable mission within the military means available a decade ago, conditions have since changed to make its successful execution extremely doubtful. Our allies have never regained their pre-World War II strength and, despite our prodding them to make their contingents truly combat-worthy, they have remained generally apathetic. As a result, NATO units are frequently understrength, short of modern weapons and equipment, and located at a considerable distance from their combat stations. The logistic problems of the alliance are enormous, arising primarily from the absence of an integrated logistic system capable of supporting the entire front and the lack of standardized ammunition and major equipment common to all national contingents. The American forces in southern Germany are at a particular disadvantage because of the vulnerability of their line of communications, which runs northward to Bremerhaven and the Channel, parallel with and dangerously close to the defensive front.

In contrast, the Soviet and satellite forces readily available for an attack are superior in numbers, better equipped with modern weapons, and backed by a deep communication zone. They could mount an offensive very strong in armor with little warning while their bombers and missiles rendered inoperable European ports and airfields essential to resupply from the United States. Taking into account also the strong Soviet submarine forces likely to operate in the Atlantic, one must conclude that reinforcement from the United States after the initiation of hostilities would be very costly if not impossible.

Under such conditions, it is my judgment that a major offensive would probably succeed in overrunning the NATO front and thereby permit a Soviet occupation of most of Western Europe—unless early in the conflict our side authorized the use of tactical nuclear weapons. In that case, the outcome would be unpredictable and a gamble for both sides. The Soviet Union, hoping to seize the assets of Europe intact, might halt and parley—or it might respond with tactical nuclear weapons of its own. At some point, the Allies might capitulate or, *in extremis*, the United States might counterattack with strategic weapons against Soviet targets. None of these outcomes promises success to the United States in achieving its primary objective of preventing Soviet domination of Western Europe and retaining a favorable regional balance of power—an unhappy situation attributable in large part to our continuation of a dangerous forward strategy at the enemy frontier with inadequate military means to support it.

Happily I do not expect a military catastrophe to occur, for much the same reason that I regard a strategic nuclear attack on the United States as highly unlikely. Even if a Warsaw Pact offensive were initially successful, the subsequent events depicted above would entail many risks for the Soviet Union, including that of escalation to strategic warfare and the destruction of virtually everything of value to the Soviet Union in Europe. Other lesser but still serious liabilities would include the danger of a hostile Chinese reaction on the eastern front, extensive war damage in the satellites and NATO countries even if only nonnuclear weapons were employed, and the vast problems arising from a prolonged occupation of Western Europe. Among the latter would be the difficulty of feeding the peoples of this food-deficient region without access to the grain markets of the Western Hemisphere. Faced with such risks, the Soviet Union would probably prefer to let time and internal weaknesses bring down the decadent democracies with their assets undamaged and ripe for spoliation.

The foregoing analysis indicates to me that our present military contribution does not fulfill the national purpose of making NATO defensible by nonnuclear means. Yet, while inadequate for a prolonged defense, it is unnecessarily large to serve as a symbolic American presence capable only of a trip-wire defense. Finally, the formidable disabilities of the alliance, many stemming from political, geographic, and logistic factors that cannot be quickly corrected, argue against any increase in the size of our NATO forces, already amounting to about one-third of our combat-ready army. To lose those forces at the outset of hostilities would be to suffer a loss comparable to that sustained by Great Britain when most of its professional army was destroyed in the early weeks of World War I.

My conclusion is not that the situation in Europe is untenable and that we Americans should come home in despair and write off our principal alliance. Strictly speaking, no position is untenable until attacked, and NATO will not be attacked if it continues to threaten the enemy with heavy losses and unacceptable risks. Hence we are still justified, I believe, in keeping a strong contingent in Europe (at about present strength but no larger) while we endeavor to enhance its deterrent effectiveness by improving troop dispositions and modernizing weapons and equipment. By such means we may reasonably hope to reinforce the unattractiveness of the offensive option for our enemies and thus increase the odds that the Soviet Union will choose to bide its time and await western self-destruction.

Meeting a Challenge in the Middle East or Africa. Another possible task for the armed forces would be to conduct military operations in the eastern Mediterranean or the Persian Gulf. Here they would operate under serious disadvantages, including the presence of large Soviet forces in the Mediterranean close to their home base of power, our lack of allies and bases, and our distance from home. While important interests in the region thoroughly justify a strong air and naval presence, these adverse conditions argue with equal force against any involvement of U.S. ground forces beyond the scale of, say, the Lebanon expedition in 1958. This is another part of the world where we would be wise to avoid or minimize political commitments which may require military support.

As to the ability of our forces in time of nominal peace to protect our trade from acts of economic warfare and international terrorism, much would depend on the location and internal conditions of our principal trading partners. While the protection of markets and sea lanes in the Western Hemisphere and, to a lesser degree, in the Southwest Pacific could be carried out without too much difficulty, the maintenance of access to markets in the Middle East and sub-Saharan Africa might pose serious problems depending upon Soviet behavior and local conditions within individual countries. In Africa, both the Soviet Union and China have been active for years and have acquired knowledge of the region and experience in cultivating local leaders. More recently, Cuba has appeared in force on the scene as a military arm of Soviet policy, and is now represented in thirteen nations including Ethiopia—the latter a nation with considerable potential as a second source for Soviet-controlled military manpower. Concurrently the Soviet Union has obtained port or base facilities in Guinea-Bissau, Angola, and Mozambique and is casting a longing eye on Djibouti.

Despite the geographical and political handicaps of this region, events may force a more active role on our government than prudence would justify. The guerrilla warfare rampant in Angola, southern Zaire, and on the frontiers of Rhodesia may lead to higher levels of violence and eventually involve South Africa in a large-scale racial conflict. The Soviet switch of clients from Somalia to Ethiopia and the heavy reinforcement of the latter with military equipment and Soviet-Cuban advisers is causing great concern over the possibility of expanded warfare including neighboring states like Egypt and the Sudan. It also raises the prospect of firm Soviet control established over the Red Sea and its approaches. At some point, the temptation for our leaders to take positive action will be strong, but they must not forget that our capability for military response in this region depends on the use of American forces far from home without base support—an unattractive option for those exposed to the experience of Vietnam.

Correcting the Imbalance

In this review we have noted that the ability of our armed forces to support American policy effectively is subject to severe limitations, and that their overall adequacy in most cases is very doubtful. The basic causes of this inadequacy can readily be found. In recent years, the goals of national policy have expanded, the opposition and obstacles to them have increased, and our military means have contracted. The logical remedy would be to trim our goals, reduce the opposition, increase our military means, or adopt some combination of these alternatives, any one of which would be difficult to carry out. It would be painful to retreat from political commitments already made. We cannot compel the Soviet Union to disarm, to order its navy back into coastal waters, or to abandon its interventions in Africa and elsewhere in the Third World. Singlehanded, we cannot revitalize our allies and bring them to play a more effective role in counterbalancing the growing Soviet strength. Nor can we abandon them because of their weaknesses and their geographic vulnerability. Finally, we cannot quickly or easily win the enduring affection of Third World countries, long regarded as peripheral to our interests.

Nonetheless, there are many things which can and should be done to correct the dangerous imbalance which has arisen between policy aspirations and military capabilities. The most obvious course would be to increase the conventional forces contributing to the protection of sea lanes and market regions from the dangers we have forecast. This would call for a substantial expansion of the antisubmarine and surface-control forces of the Navy and of the Army-Air forces which provide the military means for protecting land areas. These latter forces should include specially trained counter-terror units capable of preventing piracy or international terrorist activities committed against American nationals or interests and of executing reprisals or rescue operations when prevention fails.

Such an expansion of conventional forces would require new bases in regions including the South Atlantic, the Southwest Pacific, southern Africa, and the approaches to the Persian Gulf. In this last area, while the development of Diego Garcia will be of some assistance, it will by no means offset the Soviet Union's achievement in establishing shore installations along the tanker routes from the Persian Gulf around Africa.

For our strategic forces, I would propose no increase in size but a sustained effort to maintain our technological superiority over the Soviet Union while always retaining an invulnerable destructive capacity sufficient under all conditions to neutralize, paralyze, or destroy any likely Soviet target system.

If asked to estimate the cost of effecting the force modifications suggested, I could answer only in generalities. The political cost would include the restoration of some form of conscription since the present all-volunteer system will never support combat operations of any significant size or duration. As for the financial outlays, I would estimate the annual military budget required at about 8 percent of the gross national product over several years. Although well above the current level of roughly 5.7 percent, this figure does not appear excessive when compared to the 11–13 percent believed to be the Soviet outlay or the 8 percent of our own 1964 budget, the last before our involvement in combat in Vietnam.

While improving our military capabilities, we should seek to acquire economic allies able and willing to enter into long-term contracts to provide us with essential imports. An initial task would be for our diplomats, supported by economic and military advisors, to determine which countries would be most valuable to us as trade partners. Preference in this case would be determined by the nature and quantity of the products of a given country, its geographical accessibility, and its record of reliability in commercial relations.

Once these preferred countries had been identified, we would seek ways to assure durable trade relations capable of surviving variations in world price levels and the political differences certain to arise from time to time between ourselves and our suppliers. To this end, we shall need formal agreements with many Third World countries comparable to economic alliances and cemented by reciprocal advantage. For such allies, the advantage would be an assured export market for raw materials at fair and stable prices, paid in hard currency, dollar credits, food, manufactures, or items of advanced technology. For us, the advantage would be a continuing flow of the imports needed to satisfy the voracious appetite of our national economy.

But even if we were successful in increasing our forces and acquiring reliable overseas suppliers, we would still lack the political freedom of action we enjoyed in the halcyon days of our postwar preeminence. Then, as the principal victor in World War II, we benefited from the prestige and perquisites of unchallenged world leadership derived from our undisputed nuclear, naval, and economic supremacy. Assured of control of the seas, our leaders had ample means to undertake the protection of the free world and the containment of militant communism by a forward deployment of forces on the frontiers of our ideological foes.

But times have changed and many of the advantages which permitted this ambitious policy have dwindled or vanished. In strategic nuclear weapons, we can claim no more than essential parity with the Soviet Union. Our sea control no longer extends unchallenged across the oceans to the coasts of Eurasia. Whereas until quite recently we talked (fatuously I thought at the time) about an ability to conduct one and one-half or two and one-half concurrent wars, now we are uncertain of the future ability of our Navy, even if reinforced as herein proposed, to support protracted land operations in NATO while maintaining access to essential overseas markets. We are no longer a global power able to project and maintain military power wherever in the world we choose. In fact, we can claim unqualified military supremacy only in the Western Hemisphere, its coastal waters, and its principal sea approaches. If tempted to venture farther from home for purposes which might evoke serious military opposition, we should proceed with caution as we draw farther from our hemispheric power base and nearer that of the Soviet Union and its allies.

This acceptance of the limitations placed upon military power by time, space, economics, and logistics is an indication not of timidity, I hope, but of prudence based upon the experience of limited wars in Korea and Vietnam and reinforced by reflection upon changing political, economic, and social conditions at home and among our allies. It represents a mature realization that national security henceforth requires the protection of assets and interests from a broad range of threats, many of which are not military, and in so doing we must be prepared to use all forms of national power in proper combination.

These are some of the considerations which should be carefully weighed by proponents of any national policy that might require military support. They will do well to recognize that, since the military requirements of a course of action can never be nicely calculated in advance, it is the part of wisdom to avoid staking the national interest on a policy that cannot when necessary be defended by force of arms. While policy need not always go forth cap-a-pie in shining armor, it should never be seen so lightly armed as to appear incapable of martial deeds.

2

UNITED STATES GRAND STRATEGY FOR THE NEXT TEN YEARS

Bruce K. Holloway

Grand strategy has been variously defined. In this paper, the summary proposition around which the beliefs and arguments revolve is "the plan by which all elements of a society's power are used to support its security objectives."[1]

Much has been said in the past decade about deterrence. The will to deter a nuclear attack on ourselves or our allies has paced most of our military thinking. Indeed, ever since the Monroe Doctrine, the objective of our national strategy has been to deter the loss of our way of life. So far, we have been successful. The keynote for a global strategy for the United States for the next ten years will continue to be survival—but today survival is far from assured.

The Elusive Strategy of the Nonaggressor

Our national strategy is designed for our security and prosperity under the terms and objectives of the Constitution and the Declaration of Independence. Because it changes and because it is never written down in a single document, it is hard to define in detail. Moreover, it suffers from the indiscipline that is endemic to democracy. Its weakness is a dearth of advance planning compounded by imperfect adherence to such planning as does occur.

Most of all, perhaps, our national strategy is hampered by the lack of a clear-cut set of objectives that can be well understood by everyone. We have no territorial ambitions, no five-year plans, no budgets which can be counted on for more than a year at a time; our foreign policy is often one of reaction and expediency. This lack of

[1] For an interesting recent discussion of the subject, see John M. Collins, *Grand Strategy: Principles and Practices* (Annapolis, Md.: Naval Institute Press, 1973).

simple, meaningful objectives is perhaps the main reason why it is so difficult to get the U.S. citizen to worry about strategic problems, for, though they vitally affect the common good, they are beyond the realm of his daily concerns.

The Art of the Possible

Anyone who would prescribe policies for the future should have a vivid sense of the art of the possible. In the turbulent twentieth century, the difficulty of forecasting national policies has been amply demonstrated. Who, for example, in 1937 could have foreseen the Japanese attack on Pearl Harbor? Who, even among the very few who knew of the Manhattan Project, foresaw the vast complexities that atomic weapons would precipitate in the conduct of international relations?

Military Considerations. In contemplating merely the military aspects of national defense for the next decade, it would appear that the defense budget will not substantially increase. Neither will the percentage of the budget for personnel costs (now about 58 percent) appreciably decline. The draft will not be reinstituted, and any form of universal military training will probably at best be only debated. We may have military unions, but it is assumed here that this will not happen.

In recent years, inflation and indecision have skyrocketed the cost of modern military weaponry. Inflation will continue, but it must be hoped that indecision will not. One of our military policy options is better planning. Administrations must rise above the expedient attitudes, often based on inadequate experience of rapidly rotating staffs and officials, and achieve a higher degree of stability in the projection of military requirements; they must do a better job of selling these to the Congress and the people, and—barring large-scale conflict—they must stick to their projections. We have established a very alarming pattern of getting less and less for more and more, and we can work toward reversing this pattern through increased trust and respect for the advice of the military professional and a better job on the part of the military professional in selling his product all the way up the line of budgetary review.

Another option we have is greater attention to innovation. At a time when the enemy seems to be gaining in terms of both weaponry and force structure, there is surely a tremendous premium on figuring out how to do things better. While the age-old fire and movement principles have not changed, modern military innovations in tactics have been real advances. The German blitzkrieg and the Inchon landings are cases in point. Technical innovation to meet immediate tactical needs in Vietnam is another. We finally figured out how to build bulls-eye weapons which reduced the cost of target destruction tremendously, and we responded magnificently with new electronic countermeasures which were very effective against the finest anti-aircraft system ever encountered in war.

Another closely related option is greater emphasis on force and weapon system flexibility. During World War II, the P-51 was almost passed up but turned out to be the best fighter aircraft of all time. It performed all the jobs of tactical aircraft better than any other fighter on either side could do any one of them. It was the epitome of air-weapon flexibility in its day. We tried to recapture the same flexibility in the jet age with the F-111 and would probably have succeeded to an appreciable degree but for the major design and mission changes directed by the secretary of defense. The B-1 also promises great mission flexibility—especially in its projected specialty, supporting general purpose forces where there is a sudden requirement for heavy and accurate fire power out of the immediate range of all other friendly forces. It is hard to imagine a deliverer of high weapon tonnages with greater flexibility of application than a modern long-range bomber such as the B-1. Let us hope that the presidential decision to cancel its production will be reconsidered.

These are basic military policy options which bear on the shaping of a realistic grand strategy. They are certainly not as optimistic as those we entertained fifteen years ago, but in those fifteen years the national outlook has changed tremendously.

Foreign Affairs. Is human rights our international banner? Does it lie at the heart of a millenium that we seek to bring about for the whole world? Is it our equivalent of the Communists' goal of world conquest or, as they call it, "world liberation"? If it is, the time for aggressive enforcement is not now. It is not a viable bargaining issue from our current position in world affairs.

At times our allies have scoffed at the naiveté with which the United States conducts its foreign relations. To a considerable extent, this criticism is deserved. We are in many cases pseudo-moralists, who act selfishly when the chips are down. We are poker players who play each hand as it comes, usually without any long-term strategy. We tackle each problem singly and head-on, expecting to solve it immediately.

Just three decades ago, the United States forced a coalition between Mao Tse-Tung's Communists (Agrarian Reformers) and the

Kuomintang by threatening to remove our support from the Chiang government if it did not comply. The principal apparent reason for this was American distaste for warlord rule, which we deemed immoral and inefficient by our standards. We took precipitate action. The result was the communization of the most populous nation in the world except for the small fraction that managed to escape with Chiang to Taiwan. By projecting our code of morals, we brought down the curtain on 700 million friends. Their system was 4,000 years old; ours 170. How much better to have held to a more patient course and avoided any ultimatum based on a determination that our system was automatically right and theirs wrong.

Somewhat later we performed a similar operation in Cuba, and still later we engaged in a political maneuver in Vietnam that led to the most incredibly misdirected combatant effort of national scale in modern history. Except in Europe, our record is not good.

Patience and diplomatic tolerance for the beliefs and systems of friendly governments—even when we believe them morally wrong—are vitally needed in the negotiation of foreign policy.

Another weakness in the conduct of our foreign affairs—and a related one—is myopic and specious analysis of enemy goals, strategy, and methodologies. Our relations with the Soviet Union are filled with examples, going all the way back to President Truman's alleged statement about "Good old Joe—I know how to get along with him."

In evolving our military strategy of assured destruction (an assumed capacity for casualties and industrial damage inflicted in retaliation which would deter strategic nuclear attack) which originated in the 1960s, we seem to have assumed that the Kremlin has the same cultural values that we have; and in particular that assured second-strike damage levels of x millions of dead and y billions of economic destruction would be sufficient to deter the Soviet Union from entertaining thoughts of a massive strike against ourselves and/or our allies. Even a quick perusal of the *Communist Manifesto* of the principles of dialectic materialism, or—more importantly—of the record should be enough to convince us otherwise. There is little categorical distinction at governmental levels in the Soviet Union between the value of people and things. Some people have more value than others and some things more than others. Some things have more value than some people, and vice versa. War in Europe has been deterred not by our threat of assured destruction but by the overall superiority—until recently—of U.S. military power.

The one area where we have conducted a generally sound and consistent foreign policy over the past thirty years is Western Europe. This is fortunate, because it could well be argued that this is the most important region for us. The creation of NATO and the Marshall Plan were far-sighted, based on the simple but sagacious tenet of grand strategy that the futures of the United States and Western Europe are inextricably tied not only as a matter of geopolitical security, but also as a matter of economic interdependency.

Many times our lion's share of NATO support has come under internal political attack. For the most part, the attack centers on our military force structure in Supreme Headquarters Allied Powers, Europe (SHAPE) and the costs of its maintenance. Our contribution is several times larger than that of any other NATO member, and hence the question continues to arise, Why cannot they do more? The question is moot, but the best evidence to date is that if the United States made substantial military withdrawals from Europe, the difference would not be made up by further commitments of other members. We should continue to press for heavier commitments, as our current administration is now doing, but we should also always remember that if Western Europe falls, so, in more or less rapid sequence, will the United States.

In Asia the big issue for the next decade is, of course, Communist China. Given the cheerful nature of the Chinese people, their intense family loyalty, and their fundamental strength of individual character, it is difficult to visualize these people under totalitarian communism. Nevertheless, there are no signs of the regime's weakening. The China of World War II is no more, and in its place is a doctrinaire state locked in major racial and political conflict with the Soviet Union, yet still a Communist state that envisions a future world of socialism of which China will eventually be the epicenter.

Full diplomatic relations with the People's Republic of China are not in our best interests, and we have no need for formal pacts of cooperation. It is surely true that, at least for now, there is agreement between the People's Republic and ourselves that the greatest enemy of each is the Soviet Union, and this is a security advantage for both nations. It is possible that the People's Republic might become a second front in a Soviet war with Western Europe, and the United States a co-respondent—economically, logistically, or otherwise—in a major attack against China. But there the advantages end, and they are transitory.

Favorable trade relations are what China wants most from us. We have much to offer the Chinese in closer and freer trade, with food, raw materials, technology, and industrial management heading the list. China can offer essentially nothing that would be of substantial advantage to us through such agreements. We should drive hard bargains; place carefully controlled sanctions against exportation of such commodities as advanced technology, industrial equipment, and production management systems; and place all trade on a strict cash and carry basis. Beyond this, we should do little other than encourage tourism and such types of cultural exchange as might promote a better understanding of what is happening within China's sphere of totalitarian control.

Above all, the United States should continue to support our proven friends and allies in Asia—Taiwan, South Korea, and Japan—and should never offer any indication that we might accept, or even acknowledge "one China," the condition the Communists have set for closer diplomatic ties.

Energy

Since the Spanish American War, the United States has been accorded without dispute the status of a world power, and since World War I, it has been generally regarded as the leader of the western world. We may not have started the industrial revolution, but we provided the principal ingredients which made possible its fantastic acceleration: the technology, the technical adaptation, the structural materials, the mass production techniques, transportation, and above all Yankee ingenuity. We also spearheaded the transformation of energy dependence in the western world, if not in the whole of the civilized world, from wood and coal to oil. We did this in large part by making the automobile, the truck, and the airplane absolute essentials of the western economy. Industry is overwhelmingly dependent upon oil, and national defense is even more so. Now the future availability of oil is about to present us with the gravest crisis we have ever faced.

As a potential weapon of economic warfare, oil is without parallel in civilized history. This is so, ironically, because the heaviest consumers own or control the smallest remaining reserves and because the lines of supply from the fields upon which our dependence grows ever greater are long and terribly vulnerable. As the Soviet Union makes steady gains in port treaties, base rights, and installations from the Persian Gulf southward along the east coast of Africa and helps to precipitate territorial problems throughout Africa, this vulnerability takes on ever sharper focus.

For the past four years, there has been considerable discussion about new energy programs for the United States, but not much action. It is true that during this time we have built the trans-Alaska pipeline and made conditions somewhat more favorable for offshore drilling, but these are holding actions. We need drastic relief in the form of other sources of useful energy. The time for action is now. The lead times are long and the percentage of our oil that is imported is steadily rising despite efforts to increase the availability of domestic petroleum.

One has only to recall the Ploesti raids of World War II and other Allied attacks on the German petroleum supplies to realize what can happen here in the next ten years if a shortage of oil suddenly becomes critical. As Albert Speer points out in *Spandau Diaries,* the effort of the Third Reich to produce synthetic fuel came too late, was too small in scale, and—most importantly—depended on the availability of significant amounts of petroleum and other critical materials.[2] It provided only minor and temporary relief.

If our oil supply were appreciably curtailed, perhaps the most serious result would be an immediate reduction in our military effectiveness. Our ability to make use of the weapons of war would dwindle almost to nothing and the problem of apportioning the nation's petroleum resources would become a political dilemma of frightening proportions. How much would be held for the strategic reserve stockpile? Would deterrence come to be thought of as a luxury, compared with the demands of the economy? Then again, if our oil supply were severely curtailed as a result of Soviet sea lane interdiction, how could we respond?

The game of "what if" is very appropriate here.

- What if the Russians imposed a military blockade on tanker shipping along the east coast of Africa?

- What if we tried to break such a blockade and were handed an ultimatum that the Soviet Union would enforce it with whatever degree of military force were necessary?

- What if we had done nothing to improve our fighting navy and conventional air power and actually found ourselves without the military means to break the blockade and keep the sea lanes open?

- What if we had made good progress in sea power but had allowed our overall strategic power to deteriorate even further than it has already relative to that of the Soviet Union, and the enemy held to its ultimatum—what would we do?

---

[2] Albert Speer, *Spandau—The Secret Diaries,* trans. by Richard and Clara Winston (New York: MacMillan, 1976).

President Carter showed foresight and courage in the energy proposal he recently presented to the Congress. It was, as anticipated, a political bombshell. Some of its provisions may have been ill-advised, but it was a strong plan that properly underscored the overriding importance of tackling our energy problem for both the immediate and the long term. The President was quite right to compare the urgency of our energy crisis to that of war.

Before one has gone very far in assessing the options, some interesting but discouraging answers emerge. First, it seems fairly clear that the weapons of war themselves—the airplanes, tanks, trucks, and other mobile systems of high consumption—cannot within reason be converted to an entirely different form of fuel within ten years. Second, no large-scale conversion of office and domiciliary heating and cooling is just around the corner. There simply is no practicable way of storing the amount of energy required for all-year needs in most climates within the cost range of the potential consumers. Conversion to solar energy on a national scale sufficient to make appreciable reductions in our petroleum demands is not a near-term option, no matter how attractive and practicable it may be for the future, and the same applies to wind power, tide power, and oceanic differential thermal power.

Third, automobiles—all 100 million of them—cannot be converted to accommodate any fuel other than gasoline until a petroleum shortage of catastrophic proportions has occurred. The main reason is overwhelming public resistance to the cost and inconvenience that such mass conversion would entail.

So, again, what are our options? If the problem is as crucial as it appears and as the President apparently believes it to be, two options seem most promising, namely, placing overriding budgeting and industrial priority on (1) accelerated construction of fixed nuclear power plants on a nationwide scale, and (2) conversion of shale and low grade coal to liquid fuels that can be used in most industrial power systems after only minimum modifications.

There is strong evidence that the technology for both of these undertakings is at hand. Certainly the obstacles to a major nuclear power effort are not technological deficiencies but the belief that such a program would create serious health and safety hazards.

U.S. reserves of coal and shale seem almost endless, provided a practical technology for synthesizing lower grade deposits can be applied on a large scale. Research into the chemical and physical aspects of conversion has progressed enormously since the German effort during World War II, and there is rapidly growing support among the technical and industrial communities for this route as the quickest insurance against the disaster that would befall us if we really ran short of oil.[3]

Military Strategy, Doctrine, and Policy

During my service in the armed forces, I was vividly struck by the discrepancy between our professed military strategy of assured destruction and our actual policy of more compassionate treatment of the enemy in combat than has ever been known. While we promised to kill upwards of 50 million people in retaliation for a nuclear strike of any scale on ourselves or our allies, we took protracted pauses to allow the enemy in Vietnam to reconsider or regroup. We court-martialed a lieutenant for killing a few villagers who might very well have been enemy collaborators or grenadiers, and we exacted severe disciplinary measures for inadvertent damage to tactical targets not approved in Washington. This fundamental contradiction is part of what made our seven-year involvement in Indochina inexplicable to the public. It is also the paramount reason why assured destruction has lacked credibility in the eyes of the enemy.

Certainly, the overall strategic aim of the United States should be deterrence. Ours is a melioristic society dedicated to peaceful international competition and cooperation. At every step along the continuum of conflict from coercion to catastrophe, our object is to terminate the opponent's aggression. And, at every step, there must be an appropriate strategy, program, and force structure.

Fortunately, since 1972, assured destruction has given way to a much wiser strategy of flexibility. Our nuclear options have become broader, and both they and our overall program goals have been clarified. However, there are still large gaps in the strategy, and even larger gaps in the projected weapon and force structures that must match the strategy. The biggest gap is the lack of a doctrine for employment of tactical nuclear weapons. Since 1965 or thereabouts, our policy in Europe has shifted and floundered, we have moved from an exclusively nuclear standard for all general-purpose air forces, to a mixed standard, to a conventional-weapon standard, to one—today—which is perhaps best described as amorphous. The shift away from the nuclear standard was instigated by the United States over some

[3] Hans Mark, "Technology Development and the National Purpose," in *Critical Choices for Americans*, vol. 4, *Power and Security* (Lexington, Mass.: Lexington Books, 1976); and Michael I. Yarymovych, "Energy and National Readiness," paper presented to the Air Force Association Symposium on the Imperatives of National Readiness, Los Angeles, California, October 22, 1976, pp. 6–14.

very strenuous objections from our European allies. Accordingly, it is our job to fix it.

The first step might be to define our terms. The word "tactical," for example, as it applies to the weapons of war themselves has less and less meaning. The line of demarcation between tactical and strategic weapons, especially nuclear weapons, is altogether unclear. It would be much more useful to distinguish between "strategic" and "theatre" weapons. Certainly there are and will be weapons capable of both types of application; nevertheless, it makes much better sense to classify weapons according to their military use rather than to their geographic range or explosive power.

The next step, as indicated earlier in a broader context, is to examine closely Soviet military strategy and doctrine. The military services appear to have done much better in this regard of late than has been the case at higher levels of policy formulation and decision making. We are guilty, in general, however, of mirror-image analysis, and have harbored some very illogical views about the use of nuclear weapons in warfare. For example, there is no known evidence that an attack on Western Europe would be designed for widespread destruction. Why should it be? World conquest would probably require a large share of the resources of capitalistic civilization. Furthermore, if the West were destroyed, what kind of a world would be left? The "one-two punch" strategy of Russian design gives every indication of calling for shock action to reduce the means and will for waging war—and the greatest possible containment of collateral damage to all other resources. All types of weapons that could contribute would be used.

We have long held that nukes are not "just another weapon." We have vigorously and self-righteously preached this notion on moral grounds, and not without logic. However, it is time to set aside this Sunday-school doctrine in favor of the kind of hard planning that amalgamates the entire spectrum of weaponry. The place to start is in Europe, in the European Command and in SHAPE. In Washington, this shift must be recognized as necessary and encouraged.

Command Structure. The way in which the command and control of our military forces are organized is generally believed to be sound. It was well thought out from both a domestic and a combined-operations standpoint and has stood the test of time. My own experience of command responsibility at almost every level of joint and combined operations bears out this belief. Nevertheless, there are a few points that should be emphasized, and one major change that has been proposed seems desirable.

In a recently published paper on the National Security Council

(NSC), General Andrew J. Goodpaster points out that the composition and functions of the NSC have varied substantially according to the desires of the President. As Goodpaster puts it,

> a strong NSC is designed primarily to meet the needs of the President, who bears the great responsibility and performs the crucial role. The NSC should be the principal forum for policy-level deliberations, with the President participating personally and substantively (and, of course, making the key decisions). The NSC should be supported by a sub-committee structure, with representation from each of the respective departments and agencies and from the White House Staff—charged with responsibility for preparing plans and policies, supervising the coordination of operations and assuring a close correlation of major areas of effort, such as military programs, intelligence and arms control, with higher policy.[4]

The second point that should be emphasized is joint training. The Unified Command Plan is sound, and the publication of the Joint Chiefs of Staff, *Unified Action Armed Forces*, has served well over the past thirty years of peace and war for joint combatant planning and operations. In 1961, a major step forward was made with the formation of the United States Strike Command, which encompassed for operational command all general-purpose air and ground forces in the continental United States. The commander in chief, United States Strike Command (CINCSTRIKE), was given strong responsibilities and authority for the formulation of joint doctrine for air/ground operations and for the joint training of all forces in the zone of interior committed to such operations. It was highly successful, and for the four years prior to our involvement in Vietnam, thanks in the main to the imagination and leadership of its first commander, General Paul D. Adams, much progress was made through a series of both small- and large-scale tactical exercises combined with a great deal of paper exercise-type research and innovation. Since that time, Strike Command has been replaced by Readiness Command; its joint operational responsibilities are essentially unchanged, but its institutional and budgetary support and the environmental restraints imposed upon its work are new. It is no longer possible to conduct exercises outside of a military reservation, for example, and often not even on certain parts of these. We badly need to return to the spirited and effective joint training of all U.S. general-purpose forces that was the practice in the early 1960s.

[4] Andrew J. Goodpaster, "Four Presidents and the Conduct of National Security Affairs—Impressions and Highlights," *Journal of International Relations*, vol. 2, no. 1 (Spring 1977), p. 26.

The major change that has been proposed is the formulation of a strategic command. A most pronounced incongruity of policy and organization control vis-à-vis the Unified Command Plan (UCP) and the national mandate of direct presidential execution of the Single Integrated Operational Plan (SIOP) for the employment of U.S. strategic nuclear forces is the fact that these forces are apportioned among and controlled by five separate military commanders. The preponderance of force is under the Strategic Air Command (SAC), but the unified commands of the Pacific (PAC), Atlantic (LANT) and Europe (EUCOM) control appreciable portions in their respective regions, and the Continental Air Defense Command (CONAD) controls—such as they are—the strategic defense forces.

In 1969, the President's Blue Ribbon Committee for Defense Reorganization recommended a strategic command, but proposed that it be superimposed between the above-mentioned commands and the Joint Chiefs of Staff. The committee's reasons for recommending this additional layer are not clear, but they appeared to be political. Whatever the reasons, this author believes the proposal to be sound and wise but the superimposition unnecessary. Not only is the mission very cohesive in nature, but also the hardware, circuitry, and management-of-control apparatus are extremely critical to decision followed with instantaneous execution. All of the forces of SAC, and the nuclear strategic forces of LANT and PAC, could constitute the strategic command. Since CONAD is interlinked with the North American Air Defense Command (NORAD), and EUCOM forces are affiliated with SHAPE planning, their assignment would probably require some type of conditional operational command arrangement.

A good, simple way to begin streamlining control of our strategic forces would be to establish a direct command link between "Looking Glass" and the strategic forces of LANT and PAC. Looking Glass is the airborne command post of SAC, which is continually on station and which, in the event of nuclear attack on the United States, would have a very good chance of survival. If necessary, LANT and PAC representatives could be accommodated aboard.

The Problems of NATO. In assessing overseas military requirements, we should look sharply at several problem areas in NATO. Our allies in Western Europe are still our most important overseas investment. As a matter of national security, they are no less important than they have ever been, but they have grown weaker with respect to the Iron Curtain countries in several ways. The Warsaw Pact could mount an attack at any time which would be very difficult to stop.

SHAPE needs better equipment of all kinds, and more of it—in place. Reinforcing SHAPE with units from the United States would be to no avail if the forward wall of NATO could not hold. This applies especially to ground units, but it is true of many air units as well. Only those which could move at a time of increasing tension would be useful, and even then, unless matching logistic support were available, organized, and secured on the continent, their effectiveness would be marginal.

Nowhere is the maintenance of an advanced state of alert for any kind of attack more necessary than it is in Western Europe. Forces must be there, combat ready, coordinated, and served by a standardized and integrated command control system. For many, many years, the standardization of command control, of operating procedures, and of supply logistics has been regarded as urgent business in Europe. Some worthy progress has been made in operations, as well as in certain logistics matters, but much more is needed. Ammunition, for example, should be completely standardized, as should, insofar as possible, engines, wheels, brakes, and other common vehicular parts.

Control procedures and communications head the list of functional military services needing standardization within the SHAPE force and command structure. Although the establishment of the Central Air Region was a significant step, allied forces still operate with different combatant equipment, communications equipment, operational and logistic procedures, and control systems. Standardization and interoperability within both air and ground elements can pay tremendous dividends in the force readiness and combat potential of SHAPE. A priority effort in this direction would do much to overcome the discouraging quantitative force disparity between NATO and the Warsaw Pact and the ever-improving quality of Warsaw Pact equipment.

Other vital ingredients of an overhaul of NATO's strategy include: (1) a higher state of alert; (2) committed forces in place, with properly balanced and dispersed ready logistic support; (3) an expanded structure of small operating bases for tactical air units; and (4) integrated weapons planning and a doctrine for the employment of theatre nuclear weapons.

Top Priorities: Weapons and Mobility. Turning to the world arena at large, weapons accuracy and reliability and force mobility on a global scale are the most important of all the factors that will shape our operating doctrine and tactics in the ten years ahead. Nothing underlines this more starkly than the absolute indispensability of oil to our security. A very sizable and growing portion of our oil is imported over 8,000-mile routes where friendly bases are few and far between.

Until we can greatly reduce this dependence, absolutely top priority must go to the forces, weapons, and supporting systems that could meet a challenge to our supply lines. The current weaknesses are glaring: the deterioration of our fighting navy, of our long-range strike aircraft, and of our overseas operating bases.

The United States Navy's classic mission is to keep the sea lanes open. It is ill equipped to do this. While the ballistic missile submarine forces have been expanding and modernizing, the conventional fighting force has been steadily declining. The number of large combat surface ships has declined by more than 40 percent over the past decade and is now down to approximately 185 ships of varying states of obsolescence; the number of attack submarines has dropped 10 percent to a total of about 95.[5] The submarine fleet is scheduled to increase with the addition of modern nuclear subs, but the numbers, rate, and priorities are unknown. It appears that if present trends continue, the ratio of Soviet to U.S. combatant ships will be approximately as follows by 1985:

- major surface combatants, 1.2 to 1,
- nuclear powered attack and cruise missile submarines, 1.5 to 1, and
- nonnuclear powered submarines, infinity, or about 180 to 0.[6]

Although we still have thirteen aircraft carriers, their vulnerability is steadily increasing, and a greater and greater complement of air power would be required in combat just to keep them afloat.

High speed surface combatants and submarines with modern cruise missiles of devastating power and accuracy, together with long-range aviation of similar fire power capabilities, would appear to be the most effective armaments for protecting the sea lanes in the immediate and proximate future.

The B-52 is the only aircraft which currently fits this role, but it is—like the aircraft carrier—becoming more and more vulnerable. Fighter bases are simply nonexistent within range of most of the long supply routes in question, and the amount of tanker support needed to get these fighters to remote scenes of action—and back—would be exorbitant. The combination of surface destroyers, submarines, and aircraft, however, is especially attractive, with the long-range offensive aircraft comprising that element which could arrive first with shock action at the scene of surprise attack or harassment.

[5] *Congressional Record*, Senate, August 5, 1977, p. S14089.

[6] John S. Foster, Jr., "Military Aspects of Change, National Security, and Peace," *Critical Choices for Americans*, vol. 4, *Power and Security*, p. 164.

The charge, made recently, that the B-1 costs as much as an aircraft carrier is not true. As expensive as it has become by virtue of budget cuts, changes in specification, top-level indecision, and inflationary trends, the B-1 is a weapon we can ill afford to shelve. Its many virtues as a member of the strategic forces Triad have been aired over and over—together with the fundamental point that if we need a bomber, we surely need a new one. Here I would only add to the debate a point that has been little discussed either in the media or in the processes of federal budget review, namely, the tremendous potential of a fast, versatile, long-range, very heavily armed aircraft which can deliver various types of firepower in contingencies anywhere in the world from home bases on very short notice. Our need for such a plane could suddenly become poignantly real. Given the speed, the range, the defensive systems and equipment, the manned crew, and the very large payload capacity of variegated modern weaponry of the B-1, it is hard to imagine a more versatile and flexible weapon. Surely it is not too late to reconsider the cancellation of B-1 production and to emphasize the multitude of important roles beyond its primary mission which this modern bombardment aircraft could fill so admirably. It would be the high-scorer at a time when strategy is more and more dependent on weapon system flexibility.

Points of Primacy

The Pacing Role of Technology. Technology drives military strategy. Throughout history—since the battle of David and Goliath and before—it always has. Gunpowder, grapeshot, the French 75, the B-17, the tank, the aircraft carrier, the B-29, and the atomic bomb: all are highpoints in the progressive adaptation of strategy to technological breakthrough.

It has never been the other way around, but in the United States today, we would do well to ponder the disturbing evidence of forces that attempt to change this axiomatic principle of military science and progression. Vietnam, unbalanced SALT agreements, and opposition to the improvement of ballistic missile accuracy all suggest this trend. To thinking people everywhere who value freedom, this should be a sobering thought, for it is a specious trend that can bring the most tragic consequences.

Until recently, the most accurate of all military weapons was the infantry rifle. Its superiority was not related to design or workmanship, but rather to the fact that it made use of the human eye, which was the most accurate of all sighting and gunlaying devices. Technological advancement came first in electromechanical aids for the eye, in the form of lead computers for moving targets, mechanical bomb sights, quick read-out distance-measuring attachments, and the like. More recently, high-resolution radar, infrared, and other types of homing equipment (to include laser applications) have made possible the fabrication of weapons with absolute accuracy against almost any conceivable type and position of target. The old days of artillery adjustment—the gradual reduction of "overs" and "shorts" until a hit was finally made if the target stayed still long enough—are gone.

This is a revolutionary change of the first order. No longer should it be necessary to specify required and desired terms of accuracy in writing formal military requirements. Every weapon fired should make a direct hit. Together with large advances in reliability and the power of conventional explosives, direct-hit accuracy makes possible a truly new world of potential for ground, naval, and air forces and can, if comprehended and projected wisely, result in advances in the doctrine, composition, and tactics of warfare which will make old and more cumbersome methods obsolete. Anti-tank effectiveness, for example, should be immeasurably increased.

Recently, an argument has raged at the highest levels of government which surely must qualify as a classic example of idiocy. It is the argument over whether the weapons of atomic warfare should be made more accurate. We have the means to improve accuracy, and yet for reasons that are partly political and mostly obscure, there is widespread resistance to taking this "destabilizing" and "provocative" step. This strange reasoning makes as little sense in terms of deterrence as it does in terms of war fighting. If the argument was that we should unilaterally disarm, it would be more expeditious to eliminate than to merely prevent their qualitative improvement. To do otherwise would violate both economy of force—a thoroughly proven principle of war —and economy of military budget.

Basic research and technology are one thing; technical adaptation is another. We have excelled in both, and the combination, which is commonly referred to as research and development, has been the cornerstone of a rapidly changing and loosely defined military strategy. This in turn has supported an elusive national strategy. Within the strategic options that are available to us over the next decade, research and development will assume even greater importance than it has assumed in the past. If we are not going to match the enemy with equal resources, we must seek advantages in other ways. We have found them before; we must find them again, and we can if we quit trying to kill the goose which has already laid so many golden eggs. In particular, we must give top priority to providing:

(1) a better fighting navy,

(2) an improved long-range strike aircraft,

(3) better and more secure command control systems (this applies particularly to SLBM forces), and

(4) bulls-eye accuracy for all weapons.

Communication. To me, the most impressive event of the twentieth century, the one that has best confirmed my faith in the American system and the American people, was our performance from December 1941 to August 1945. Within twenty-four hours of the attack on Pearl Harbor, there was a dramatic change in attitude of our people, perhaps the most dramatic since our beginning. Suddenly there was no doubt about what we had to do. Everyone understood. There were no strikes, no talk of strikes; no griping about overtime; no isolationist headlines. Suddenly we stopped squabbling about whether or not we could afford this or that—and listened to our President asking for 50,000 airplanes.

The Japanese attack communicated with unparalleled eloquence what three years of steady and brutal German expansion, what even the invasion of Poland and the declarations of war by England and France, had failed to convey. A gifted President made the most of it, adding to the sheer power of events his own subtle understanding of persuasion and motivation.

But what, short of another Pearl Harbor, would direct the public's attention to the dangers which face our country? It seems to me that the American people would be well served and the security of the United States promoted by a national information program that might do this. In particular, it might include a weekly national television show treating critical problems of the country.

The power of U.S. television corporations is gargantuan, and abuses of reporting responsibility have increased. There have been many extremely fine documentaries on various subjects of cultural and economic interest, but the bulk of reporting tends toward sensationalism, and the character, facts, and seriousness of national problems, by and large, are not accurately represented. One of the most irritating and discouraging examples of newscasting egocentricity is the practice of having a commentator proceed immediately after a major presidential TV appearance to interpret what the President said. A nationally sponsored and nationally controlled program could avoid this and other depreciating aspects of current mass communication for all those who want and need the facts.

We surely do not want another "Pearl Harbor" to force the public's attention to the dangers which face our country. But we need something, because in our form of government, the telling is as important as the doing. If through such communicative innovation as national information programs we can achieve broader popular understanding and support and broader acceptance for the necessity of current sacrifices for a brighter future—or any future at all—we will have achieved a monumental step forward.

The Near Term

For the next decade, the two blockbuster problems are energy and defense, and they are very closely related. If we do not make the necessary effort in these two areas under a reformed national strategy of concerted action and individual sacrifice, some foreign power will solve our problems for us.

Negotiated control of the weapons of Armageddon is not enough. In the space of the next few years, there is insufficient time to achieve clear military superiority over the Soviet Union—not even if we were prepared to make the supreme industrial efforts of the 1941–1945 period. The best we can hope is to reestablish parity in the power of our strategic nuclear forces and to concentrate intense efforts on the development of conventional forces and supporting services to the point where we could not only fight decisively at all conflict levels but also—and equally important—secure vital logistics. Nowhere is this need more dramatic than in the case of oil.

Gradual conversion of automobiles from fifteen miles per gallon to twenty or twenty-five miles per gallon engines is not enough. Neither is conversion to solar heat. Massive conversion of petroleum-consuming fixed power installations to another fuel is the only promising way of diminishing our reliance on imported oil in the next few years. For the moment, the only promising options are low grade coal and shale refinement, and nuclear power.

Somehow, the people have to understand these truths. For a healthy, viable national grand strategy, what is needed above all is recognition of the problems we face, and the resolve and priority action to meet them.

3

SOVIET STRATEGY AND U.S. COUNTER-STRATEGY

Elmo R. Zumwalt, Jr.

Introduction to Strategy

An intense—at times bitter—debate rages today with regard to U.S. national strategy, the course which American policies will pursue around the world in the years ahead. As the argument develops, it exposes deep divisions both within and outside the government. People disagree about everything from the extent of the threat confronting our nation, to the strategy by which that threat should be countered, to the military force levels required to implement the chosen strategy.

Within the U.S. government the debate was sparked by Presidential Review Memorandum No. 10 (or PRM Ten, as it is known in Washington) which created a study group to solve the new President's national security problems. Or rather it created two groups. Professional military planners in the armed services were dismayed to learn that the study was to be undertaken simultaneously on two tracks: one group, headed by Professor Samuel P. Huntington, would do a "net assessment" of the threat to which the United States was currently exposed and prospects for the future; concurrently, a second group, headed by Dr. Lynn Davis, late of the Carter transition team and now deputy assistant secretary of defense for policy planning, would set about devising national strategies and military force levels. When this *modus operandi* was revealed, the question immediately posed in the corridors of the Pentagon was: How can proper strategies and supporting military force levels be determined when the threat which must be overcome has not yet been postulated? The answer, of course, is that they cannot. Instead one must infer that some other determinant governs the exercise, perhaps the budget. Those who have spent most of their lives planning and executing the defense of the United States know a far better way to study American national security problems.

First, one defines U.S. national aims and objectives. Then an assessment is made of perceived threats which might preclude achievement of these objectives. Once this assessment has been made, it is possible to devise a range of strategies, each designed to achieve the defined goals in the face of the expected opposition. Finally, one can determine the military force levels necessary to execute the selected strategy. And if the determined level of force proves not politically or fiscally supportable, if some lesser capability is elected by the governmental leaders, the planners can then estimate the national risk which must be assumed. Only with this kind of logical analysis can the nation's leaders make sound decisions about the course the nation will follow.

Soviet Strategy. My first premise is that the Soviet Union is clearly the main antagonist of the United States. If the menace posed by the Soviet Union is adequately analyzed, the strategies devised to cope with that menace are sound, and the requisite forces are fielded, the nation will be fully prepared to meet any other conceivable contingency. Should a Soviet challenge and some lesser crisis occur simultaneously, however, we would need additional forces the size of which would be determined by the severity of the second contingency.

Since today and for the foreseeable future the principal obstacle to the achievement of American goals is the Soviet Union, one must begin by analyzing Moscow's aims and objectives—specifically those that conflict with ours—and its ways of accomplishing them. So what is the Soviet Union about? Despite the euphoria which has periodically been generated in the West by the Russian-originated term peaceful coexistence and its murky successor détente, the fundamental goal of the Soviet Union has remained unchanged since the days when Nikolai Lenin told the Eighth Party Congress, in 1919: "We are living not merely in a state, but in a system of states, and the existence of the Soviet Republic side by side with imperialist states for a long time is unthinkable. One or the other must triumph in the end."[1] This basic theme has been reiterated over and over again by every Soviet leader who has succeeded Lenin, and never more bluntly than by Nikita Khrushchev when he threatened to "bury" us.

While relative military strength has been and still is a basic ingredient of the continuing Soviet-American confrontation, it would be a serious mistake to focus on this facet alone. For the Kremlin leaders obviously plan to use every method available to them in their

---

[1] *Soviet Work Outlook*, Department of State Publication 6836 (Washington, D.C.: July 1959), p. 96.

campaign to reduce the power of any nation or coalition of nations that might be capable of frustrating what Moscow perceives as the ultimate destiny of the red revolution. This is what they have done in the past and can be expected to do in the future. Though their slogans may change, as the Soviet Communists shift tactics in order to manipulate world opinion at any given time, the underlying meaning as viewed from Red Square remains singularly constant.

This is not to say that the Russians are executing a detailed, long-range plan devised years ago, one which meticulously articulates a step-by-step program for bringing about the inevitable world dominion of Soviet-led communism. This simply is not the case. As a matter of fact, on myriad occasions the Kremlin has demonstrated that its day-to-day policies are exploitive rather than creative. That is to say, Soviet leaders have always been quick to capitalize on any opportunity presenting itself, but by and large they have not been able to create conditions which could then be manipulated for gain. Still, it must be acknowledged that they have developed this exploitive capability to a rather high level, and all too often they have counted on and received the unwitting help of their intended victims.

From the outset, however, the Soviet Union has pursued a series of short-term objectives, each designed to further the long-term campaign. This is still its policy. Perhaps the most notable of these short-term objectives has been the development of a heavy industrial base. Lenin and Stalin realized early that once the Communist party had consolidated its hold on the country, they could squeeze the people as hard as necessary to turn the Soviet Union into a modern industrial state; and only such a state could produce the military prowess required to shift the "protracted conflict"—as Robert Strausz-Hupé so aptly termed it—to the battlefield when and where required.[2]

Complementing this internal drive for total self-sufficiency has been Moscow's campaign to establish, then cement, ties with those Western European countries which it was unable to seize in the aftermath of World War II. At the same time, the Kremlin seeks to alienate these nations not only from the United States, but also from the Third World. The objective is all too evident. By cutting the West off from the raw materials required to feed its industrial maw, the Communists hope to precipitate the final convulsion of capitalism predicted by Karl Marx and Nikolai Lenin.

The Kremlin seeks everywhere to cut American connections with other nations around the world, thus reducing U.S. industrial and

---

[2] Robert Strausz-Hupé et al., *Protracted Conflict* (New York: Harper & Brothers, 1959).

political power through a process of isolation. Viewing the international confrontation as a zero-sum game, the Soviet leaders calculate that every country subtracted from the U.S. orbit is automatically added to their own.

This strategy, employed through the years by the Soviet Union, is a broad one utilizing the full range of Russia's strengths and advantages. It makes use of political pressure, ideological propaganda, economic manipulation, surrogate combat troops, and in the last resort Soviet military might, all of them supported by tactical moves which can shift swiftly and dramatically. Moscow has been extraordinarily flexible in the use of tactics, depending on its international position at the moment. For instance, in the aftermath of World War II, the Kremlin—well aware of the geographic limitations to its power—mounted a comparatively modest worldwide offensive confined to ideological penetration. Acutely aware of the nuclear monopoly then enjoyed by the United States as well as recognizing the relatively limited reach of the Soviet military, constrained as it then was to crossing frontiers into countries contiguous to the motherland itself, Moscow did little more than work for the internal subversion of target nations and provide arms to prospective client states. Over the years, however, as a Russian nuclear capability evolved and especially as Russian military outreach lengthened, a far more aggressive Soviet policy emerged.

And just as quickly as the industrial base permitted, the leadership pressed for the expansion of most facets of Soviet military power. Quite understandably, Moscow assigned first priority to strategic nuclear forces. But close on the heels of this effort followed a program to provide all conventional forces across-the-board with tactical nuclear weapons. Simultaneously, these forces were expanded and modernized in other ways. Subsequently, a blue-water Soviet navy was pushed and a true sea and airborne power projection capability made an appearance. In general terms, this has been the thrust of Soviet policies up to the present, and there is abundant evidence that more of the same is in prospect. To support these assertions, we will take a detailed look at the evidence. But for the moment, given the current posture of the Soviet Union, we must ask ourselves what sort of response the United States should make.

The American Response. To begin with, of course, we must recognize that the future security and well-being of this country are threatened. All too often, this has proved to be the largest part of the problem. In some instances, the American people and their leaders have simply been unable to detect the danger arising from an international development that might damage one or more U.S. interests. In other instances, they have deliberately ignored developments they found unpalatable. The tragedy is that we have sometimes ignored threats even when our enemies told us exactly what they planned to do. There have been three striking examples of such blindness in the past five decades.

Despite the voluminous writings of Nikolai Lenin, it was not until the closing days of World War II that we came to realize that he and his political descendants meant business; by that time, of course, Lenin's successors had a sizable fraction of the national power required to make the master's predictions come true. Then there was the case of Adolf Hitler. When *Mein Kampf* (My battle), which he wrote in a German jail in 1924, was first published, few people paid any attention to the book. It did not become a worldwide best seller until the waning days of the 1930s, by which time the former Austrian house painter had solidified his control of Germany, had rebuilt the *Wehrmacht*, and was about to unleash it to fulfill the grandiose plan he had put on paper in 1924. An even less well-known but altogether similar event took place halfway around the world in the late 1920s. In Japan, the foreign minister, one Baron Tanaka, produced a document known as the *Tanaka Memorial* which outlined Japan's plans for the establishment of a greater East Asia co-prosperity sphere, an endeavor which came painfully near to permanent realization in the opening days of World War II.[3]

At first glance, it would appear that in cases like these the indifference of the citizenry was caused by their preoccupation with the present, with their own personal problems and well being; their attitude seems to have been, ignore that nasty problem and it will go away. I, for one, lay the blame at a different doorstep. In my judgment, the failure of the public to perceive an international danger in the making can be ascribed to the national leadership's reluctance or refusal to level with the American people. If the facts are clearly laid out and the dangers fully explained, the American body politic

[3] The *Tanaka Memorial* is one of the most controversial documents in recent history because the original work has never been seen outside Japan. Written in 1927, the *Memorial* submitted to the Emperor reputedly outlined a plan for world conquest. The Chinese, under Chiang Kai-Shek, pieced together segments of the *Memorial* and published them (admittedly a highly biased version). There has been considerable debate over the actual provisions of the report. Whether it allowed for world conquest is open to question; it is far more likely that it called for establishment of a "Greater East Asia co-prosperity sphere." For a balanced interpretation, see *Collier's Encyclopedia*, vol. 18 (New York: P. F. Collier & Son Corporation, 1956), p. 411.

David Bergamini, *Japan's Imperial Conspiracy* (London: Panther Books Limited, 1972), pp. 358–359, views the *Memorial* as a Chinese forgery.

will react with an unambiguous demand for whatever action might be necessary to put things right. More about this later.

Once a threat has been acknowledged, the manner of dealing with it is fairly straightforward. We need first to devise a broad national strategy which will assure the achievement of essential U.S. aims and objectives despite the threat posed by Moscow. Then we must calculate the power which will be needed to make that strategy work. Like the Soviet Union, we must marshal our disparate strengths, political, economic, ideological, industrial, technological, and military. Above all, the posture we adopt must be backed with an evident national will which clearly signals to our antagonist that we will not hesitate to employ those means whenever and wherever necessary. If this latter factor is absent, the others will carry little weight with a coldly pragmatic leadership such as that in the Kremlin.

I would characterize this approach to American security as the employment of total force. It draws into international affairs not only the strategic and conventional military and naval prowess of a nation, but also the full range of its societal and resource capabilities. The components of total force must be used in a coordinated, mutually reinforcing fashion. This is one area where we can learn from the Soviet Union, for it has proved significantly more adept at manipulating total force than have we. I will expand on this theme as we undertake a detailed evaluation of the evidence before us with regard to Soviet international machinations and what they portend for the future.

Moscow fully understands that we live in a power-political world where at bottom the international power scale comprises strategic nuclear weapons. This is where any evaluation must begin. At the outset, several things ought to be said about the strategic equation.

Beneath an umbrella of true strategic nuclear deterrence, the superpowers find themselves considerably constrained in their own freedom to initiate political as well as conventional military action. Always in the background lurks the specter of escalation to the ultimate "nuclear holocaust." Conversely, that umbrella provides significant freedom of maneuver to lesser nations. Charles de Gaulle decisively proved this thesis when he tossed NATO and the U.S. military headquarters out of France in 1966.[4] He was able to do so because he knew the United States could not retaliate by removing that segment of the American strategic umbrella which then covered France, protecting it from Soviet attack or coercion. Our only option would

[4] For a detailed discussion of this point, see Robert J. Hanks, captain, USN, "The High Price of Success," United States Naval Institute *Proceedings*, vol. 94, no. 4 (April 1968), pp. 26–33.

have been to close the umbrella on that side of the Atlantic, thus exposing all of NATO. De Gaulle well knew we simply could not take that Draconian step. The danger, of course, is that the actions of lesser nations can precipitate unsought superpower confrontations—like the U.S./Soviet face-off at the height of the Arab-Israeli war in 1973. Finally, perceptions of the strategic balance—or more accurately, imbalance—can influence the allegiance and actions of other nations, creating significant shifts of political and military power in the world, such as Finlandization. Therefore, the position of the strategic nuclear scales—actual and perceived—affects all that we do or attempt. It is vital to the future of the United States that those scales be tilted in our favor, for a critical danger arises when they become unbalanced in favor of our antagonists. Strategic nuclear superiority confers on the possessor the ability to coerce others and to achieve its purposes without firing a shot of any kind—nuclear or conventional.

From the American point of view, the history of nuclear weapons has been dreary. Starting with an unquestioned monopoly in 1945, we have—in my considered judgment—descended to the point where today our arsenal is manifestly inferior to that of the Soviet Union. Moreover, present trends suggest that the exceedingly dangerous posture in which we now find ourselves will worsen. How did the United States manage to get itself into such a fix?

After World War II the Soviet Union steadfastly declined any sort of control over nuclear weapons since it already had stolen most of the technology it needed and was well on the way to becoming nuclear capable. Following the collapse of the Baruch Plan to place international controls on the nuclear genie, the United States embarked on a program designed to provide sufficient nuclear strength to ensure our safety and that of our allies. By the mid-1960s we had fashioned a force comprising some 2,000 delivery systems. The Russians trailed us by about ten years in technology and 50 percent in numbers. At this point, we committed a cardinal error. We stopped. According to the government wisdom of the day, we had enough strength to devastate the Soviet Union should Moscow ever be stupid enough to cross the unthinkable threshold. The Kremlin would continue to build to levels something like ours, it was believed, mutual deterrence would emerge, and the "holocaust" would be foreclosed. But the Soviet leaders did not think the same way as the occupants of the Pentagon's E-ring and the oval office: the Russians continued to build. And, to them, the name of the game was "bigger is better," not only in numbers but also in size, which ultimately translates into range and throw-weight. Furthermore, with the advent of Polaris ballistic missile submarines in the United States, the Kremlin lost no time in emulating the U.S. move and soon began sending some of its own strategic nuclear force to sea. Still, we held to the magic number of 1,054 land-based intercontinental ballistic missiles and about 650 sea-launched ballistic missiles; the balance of the nation's strategic deterrent force comprised the aging B-52 bombers.

By 1972 when the first Strategic Arms Limitation Talks (SALT I) produced the Interim Agreement, putting a lid on total strategic delivery vehicles, the United States still had its 1,054 land-based ICBMs, but Moscow boasted 1,618, and these were significantly larger than the American ones.[5] For instance, the Soviet SS-9 missile—by then in silos and targeted against the United States—possessed three times the throw-weight of our own Minuteman. As if this were not enough, our advantage in ballistic missile submarines had gone down the drain as well. While the Interim Agreement permitted us 44 submarines and 710 launching tubes, the Soviet Union came away with 62 boats and a total of 950 tubes. Thus, convoluted reasoning and the administration's inordinate desire for an agreeement of any kind cemented the strategic nuclear inferiority of the United States.

The Logic of Soviet Foreign Policy since 1945

It is all too clear that neither our exemplary self-restraint nor the Strategic Arms Limitation Talks has managed to slow or inhibit in any way the Soviet drive for strategic superiority. The evidence of the continuing Russian strategic buildup is unambiguous. In addition the Soviet Union is making complementary efforts in the dispersal and hardening not only of industry but also of command, control, and communication facilities, and a huge civil defense program is under way. It should become plain to even the most casual observer that in the Kremlin, the leaders believe an all-out nuclear war *is* possible, and they believe they can win one if it comes.

No less an expert on the Soviet Union than the former director of Harvard University's Russian Research Center, Professor Richard Pipes, has explained in some detail why the Kremlin believes this to be the case.[6] Noting at the outset of a recent article that "American and Soviet nuclear doctrines . . . are starkly at odds," he charged the American strategic community with a predisposition "to shrug off this

[5] SALT I also produced the Anti-Ballistic Missile (ABM) Treaty which prohibits deployment of extensive ABM capability by either nation. The Soviets maintained their Moscow system, while we promptly dismantled the one we were building to protect our land-based ICBMs.

[6] Richard Pipes, "Why the Soviet Union Thinks It Could Fight and Win a Nuclear War," *Commentary*, vol. 64, no. 1 (July 1977).

fundamental doctrinal discrepancy." To anyone who had his eyes open during World War II, the cold war, Korea, and the rest, it sounds like Lenin/Hitler/Tanaka all over again. And it bears repeating that it is the leaders of the American government who hold these views and steadfastly refuse to present the blunt facts of the deteriorating U.S. strategic position to the American people.

If to this bleak strategic situation one adds the tactical nuclear advances being made by the Soviet Union, and then the massive effort in conventional military power, especially at sea, one finds it manifestly impossible to explain what the Soviet Union is doing except in terms of a concerted drive for global domination. It is against this background evidence that one must attempt to assess Soviet intentions—present and especially future.

On the basis of my own experience and examination, I believe the Kremlin is continuing its historic, single-minded campaign to achieve world dominion for Soviet-led communism and that it intends to be able to use any and all means at its disposal to gain that end. Inasmuch as the Soviet Union has become a "have" nation since World War II, I further believe the Russians would like very much to achieve this fundamental goal without directly engaging the Soviet Union in a war. Moscow harbors no great desire to put the motherland at risk unless the goal can be realized in no other way. When the application of military force has become necessary, the Communist leaders have employed, and will continue to use, surrogates to avoid the direct engagement of their own forces in combat. Should it ultimately prove necessary, however, they would be prepared to do the job themselves. An empirical examination of Soviet moves around the world provides revealing and informative evidence in support of this assessment of Moscow's intentions.

A Pattern of Gradually Increasing Militancy. Perhaps the best point of departure for such an evaluation is a brief review of Soviet actions from 1945 to the present. The Soviet Union emerged from World War II as the next most powerful nation after the United States. Though grievously hurt by that conflict, the Soviet Union was nonetheless the only major nation to emerge with greatly expanded borders. Unlike the other main Allied powers, it made no move to demobilize the enormous military machine it had assembled prior to and during the war years. Within the newly acquired borders of the Soviet Union as well as in Eastern Europe, Iran, and the Far East, nothing happened to match what Winston Churchill described as the melting away of the armies of democracy. Nevertheless, a serious problem stood between Joseph Stalin and the goals he sought to achieve: the limited reach of his armed forces. In 1945, only nations contiguous to the Soviet Union or occupied by the Red Army lay within the range of the Russian Bear's power. Stalin, therefore, found himself forced to concentrate on such countries as he could reach. Over the next few years, he cemented Soviet control of European nations already under the heel of the Red Army. And only the declining, but still-to-be-reckoned-with, strength of the United States and Great Britain—backed (and this is crucial) by the American nuclear monopoly—eventually forced him to withdraw from Austria and Iran. Elsewhere, despite Allied protests, Moscow proceeded to nail down its territorial gains stemming from the defeat of the Axis.

But although the might of his armed forces could not reach into the rest of the world, the Russian dictator did not by any means neglect his international aims. Militarily impotent, Stalin mounted a worldwide ideological offensive. He resurrected the international Communist infrastructure inherited from Lenin, which had lain dormant after the abrupt reversal of Russo-German relations in 1942. Stalin put this organization back to work subverting regimes around the globe. The Red Army might not be able to reach the Western Hemisphere, but ideology certainly could. And so could Soviet-manufactured arms. Carried in Russian ships, they flowed in increasing numbers to those states which seemed to be surrendering to the ideological offensive: China, Indonesia, Korea, and—to be sure—the nations of Eastern Europe.

But in the late 1940s Russian foreign policy began to change. It became noticeably more aggressive. The timing of the shift allows it to be traced directly to the emergence of a Soviet nuclear capability. Gradually Moscow increased the militancy of its thrusts, ultimately penetrating areas separated from the Soviet Union by salt water which heretofore it had been unable to influence with military power. First, however, came the confrontation over Berlin. And here one finds Moscow making the first cardinal mistake in its postwar foreign policy. Just as the embryonic European Union was beginning to recognize that it had helped to vanquish the legions of Adolf Hitler only to see them immediately supplanted by a far more powerful and implacable foe, the Russian blockade of Berlin transformed Europe into the North Atlantic Alliance and the North Atlantic Treaty Organization (NATO). Above all, it brought the United States back to Western Europe.

Then came Korea. Here the Kremlin succeeded in embroiling the entire United Nations—but most especially the United States—in the first real surrogate operation. While the Soviet military effort failed, the persistence of the Communists hardly needs elaboration when, a quarter of a century later, the issue is still a major factor in American politics and security. But the ultimate confirmation that a new nuclear power had entered center stage came in 1957. Once again, the Soviet Union proved its incredible talent for shooting itself in the political foot as it sent tanks and troops through Hungary into the heart of Budapest to eradicate signs of "counterrevolution" in the eastern bloc. Predictably, world opinion turned almost universally against Moscow, and all the propaganda gains of the past decade seemed in imminent danger of being swept away. From the American point of view, things could hardly have been better. But before the full returns could be collected, three nations—Great Britain, France, and Israel—reversed the tide: in concert, they invaded Egypt, ostensibly to safeguard the Suez Canal. Quickly Hungary was forgotten, Egypt became the focus of world opinion, and Nikita Khrushchev for the first time rattled Soviet rockets. Moscow, the aggressive, repressive predator of Hungary, had been transformed into the defender of right and justice in the Middle East. In the ensuing two decades, the West has been unable to dislodge the Kremlin from this position, and peace has largely eluded this part of the world as a result. One is constrained to observe that the Soviet Union does not have a monopoly on political ineptitude. (It is also worth noting that Khrushchev's Hungarian adventure in 1957 can well be considered the genesis of the Brezhnev Doctrine, enunciated more than a decade later in defense of the Soviet invasion of Czechoslovakia in 1968. Coming as it did when the new détente policy had just begun to bear fruit in the capitals of Europe, Moscow's swift and brutal suppression of the Czech deviationists shocked NATO into some house cleaning.)

The Growth of the Soviet Navy. In the mid-1950s an event occurred which went largely unremarked in the West but would prove to have profound ramifications. Enthralled with the power of nuclear-tipped rockets, Nikita Khrushchev decided that the Soviet navy should consist mainly of large numbers of submarines armed with "flying torpedoes." Presumably he wanted Sergei Gorshkov, whose "enthusiasm for missile technology . . . comparative youth . . . and . . . record of political reliability" appealed to him, to undertake this transformation of the navy.[7] Thus, in January 1956, Khrushchev ousted Admiral Kuznetsov as the Soviet naval commander in favor of his own protégé. But Gorshkov not only outmaneuvered his new boss, he outlasted him as well, and in the twenty-two years he has been commander in chief of the Soviet navy he has managed to forge a large, reasonably bal-

[7] David Fairhall, *Russian Sea Power* (Boston: Gambit, Inc., 1971), pp. 183–184.

anced, blue-water fleet whose surface ships are today as visible around the world as they are powerful. What would turn out to be a mistake from Khrushchev's point of view has in the long term redounded to Russian advantage.

The growing belligerency of Soviet foreign policy under Khrushchev may well have given Gorshkov the very arguments he desperately needed to convince the land-oriented Kremlin leadership of sea power's indispensable value. Although the notion is hotly contested by some in the world of academe, I believe the Cuban missile crisis of 1962 constituted a watershed in the fortunes of the Soviet navy. Sergei Gorshkov must have exploited this Russian humiliation at the hands of the U.S. Atlantic fleet with telling effect in the Kremlin councils. Whatever the actual circumstances, the results are crystal clear: the outreach of Soviet conventional military power, which was so seriously lacking during the Stalin and Khrushchev days, has now extended to the four corners of the globe in direct proportion to the growth of the Soviet navy. And that, of course, brings us to the question of where the Soviet Union stands today and how it is using this new capability.

If one peruses a world map today, one finds the Soviet Union engaged around the world, with its maritime presence—naval, merchant, fishing, hydrographic—invariably in the vanguard. From operating bases and facilities in Cuba (Cienfuegos and Havana), Russian warships and naval aircraft sit astride the myriad Caribbean shipping routes which crisscross this vital region. The Soviet navy can be found from one end to the other of the Mediterranean Sea, and its ability to contest American and allied control of its waters was frighteningly demonstrated during the 1973 Middle East war. East of Suez, the Soviet Indian Ocean squadron, which came to that area to stay in 1968, outnumbers the United States Navy most of the time and is inferior in power only during periodic U.S. carrier task force deployments to the region. In the Pacific, the pattern of Soviet operations is similar. Of supreme importance is the fact that these deployments to seas far distant from the Russian homeland are all used to demonstrate Soviet military strength which can be used to support friendly and client states as well as to intimidate those who might be currently opposing Moscow's policies. The events now unfolding in the South Atlantic and on the African continent south of the Sahara are a case in point.

To informed observers, this portion of the world is of critical significance to the West in general and to the United States in particular. American industry's dependence on raw materials imported from southern Africa is sobering. We are heavily, and in some instances completely, dependent on this region for materials such as bauxite and alumina, chromium ore, manganese ore, nickel and its concentrates, tin, tungsten, and zinc, to name but a few.[8] Myriad other materials in lesser quantities flow continuously across the South Atlantic to the United States.

Then there is the matter of oil. When the Suez Canal was shut down during the 1967 Middle East war, the sea route around the Cape of Good Hope suddenly assumed immense importance to Europe and to the United States, which had recently lost its energy independence. Closure of the canal spawned today's supertanker and, over the ensuing years, the waters south of the cape became the windy corner of the oil trade, vying for prominence with the Strait of Malacca. The significance of these heavily traveled trade routes off the southern tip of Africa and throughout the South and Mid-Atlantic did not escape the notice of the Soviet Union. Moreover, Moscow's interest in the region is not new. It did not start with Angola.

A decade ago, Moscow's heavy hand descended on the Congo following the Belgian withdrawal. The results of this effort were something less than successful. Ghana proved not much more receptive despite a heavy Russian investment in aid, military and economic. But persistence is one of the Kremlin's long suits and it eventually paid off in Guinea. Today, ships and aircraft of the Soviet navy operate routinely out of Conakry, despite the political pressure brought to bear on the regime of Marxist President Sekou Toure by the United States. And then came Angola. With introduction of Cuban combat troops—the first Communist soldiers in southern Africa—the port of Luanda joined Pointe Noire and Conakry in providing support facilities to the red fleet. Now, if one draws lines between these ports and connects them with the island of Cuba, a rough triangle is described which crosses all the shipping lanes in a major portion of the South Atlantic. By manipulating a combination of arms and economic aid, diplomatic relations and friendship treaties, Moscow seeks to cement its presence and influence in this part of the world, as well as ensuring access to facilities which will permit the Soviet Union to threaten western interests at will. The pattern is all too evident.

A Compliant Victim. As I have already suggested, the Soviet Union has been assisted in its South Atlantic endeavors by the very nations it seeks to victimize. The United States, for example, embroiled for the past two decades with Korea, Vietnam, and repeated crises in the Mediterranean, has virtually ignored the South Atlantic as well as the

[8] For an excellent discussion of this point, see Walter F. Hahn and Alvin J. Cottrell, *Soviet Shadow Over Africa*, Center for Advanced International Studies (Miami: University of Miami, 1976).

littoral nations fronting on this crucial ocean. Aside from the annual Unitas naval cruises around South America and direct transits en route to the Gulf of Tonkin and the Indian Ocean during the Vietnam era (neither of which had the political impact of a true naval presence), there has been essentially no U.S. naval activity in the area. And NATO, though critically dependent on Middle Eastern oil as well as most of the aforementioned raw materials from southern Africa, has stubbornly refused to move its Atlantic maritime boundary south of the Tropic of Cancer. Always concerned that any move to expand NATO's boundaries would inevitably increase the risk that the alliance would be drawn into one or more of the United States's worldwide commitments à la Korea or Vietnam, the member states have consistently refused to acknowledge that some NATO interests lie beyond the boundaries established decades ago. Moscow cannot help but applaud this refusal to countenance change.

A general foreign policy initiative by the United States has also aided the Soviet Union in this region. No one, of course, can fault the moral and political power of the human rights posture assumed by President Carter, especially its direct thrust at the Soviet Union. But the scatter-gun application of its tenets around the world against friend and foe alike has clearly done serious harm to American interests in several important instances. One of these impinges directly on the defense of the South Atlantic against the Russian incursion. Brazil and Argentina, historic friends and allies of the United States, are ideally located to field their own naval forces and to afford support facilities to those of the United States if the need for combat operations should arise. Furthermore, these two nations are capable of contributing to the naval presence required throughout the region to counter that of the Soviet Union. But stung by the human rights violation charges broadcast to the world by the new American administration, both nations took steps to sever the military support relationships they had maintained for many years with their neighbor to the north. Rumblings in Brazil at the time of this initial retaliatory move suggested to astute observers that the future colossus of the Southern Hemisphere might go even further. Shortly thereafter, the Atlantic fleet sent a carrier task force south for training exercises with the Brazilian navy and calls at various ports. The cruise turned out to be highly successful, and for a time it appeared that this effort had gone a long way toward repairing the damage inflicted by the human rights charges. One gesture by the U.S. Navy, however, proved not to be enough. On September 19, 1977, Brazil canceled all of its four remaining military agreements with the United States. Two of these, including a naval agreement, dated back to 1942 when the two nations undertook to cooperate against the threat posed in the South Atlantic by Nazi Germany. Given the growing Soviet influence in this region, such a rupture benefits only Moscow. We engineered it.

In sum, one cannot but wonder if control of the South Atlantic is going to go to the Kremlin by default. And if that picture is not sufficiently grim, one has only to glance at what is happening throughout the southern portion of the African continent. With the former Portuguese colony of Mozambique now in the clutches of a Marxist regime, armed and assisted to power by the Soviet Union (as was the regime in Somalia); with the same situation obtaining directly across the continent in Angola; with the cauldron stirred by the explosive black–white struggle for power in Rhodesia and South Africa—not to mention Namibia—it is not difficult to postulate violence erupting all across southern Africa as a prelude to the establishment of Moscow-backed, Marxist governments, heavily influenced by the Soviet Union and affording it access to their ports and airfields in exchange for arms and aid supplied during the struggles. Thus, commanding the windy corner off the Cape and the maritime highways of the South Atlantic proper, the Kremlin would have a double handhold around the economic and industrial throat of Europe as well as that of the United States. And if one subjects those other regions of the world where the Soviet Union is currently active to this sort of scrutiny, one discovers strikingly similar patterns. The conditions in the South Atlantic and in southern Africa, in my judgment, are symptomatic.

Total Force to Meet a Global Threat

What should the United States do about the South Atlantic threat? The quickest response, of course, would be to establish a naval presence by means of reasonably frequent naval deployments. And these should be excursions designed specifically to highlight that presence amongst the littoral nations. Aircraft carriers and our most modern surface combatants should be sent to do the job. A publicized presence of naval forces with respectable muscle, calling at friendly ports on both sides of the ocean, will reassure those nations still on our side and impress those that are either in or leaning toward the Soviet camp.

In the longer term, we need to marshal political and economic force to promote our own interests and frustrate those of the Soviet Union. For example, we ought to be less reluctant to put heat on Guinea to deny the Soviet Union access to Conakry, a port from which Soviet ships and aircraft range north and south across the

Atlantic today. At first blush it may seem inhuman to some to deny Public Law 480 food grants to any nation in order to stop it from doing that with which we take issue. Perhaps so. But on the other hand, is it fair to the American taxpayer or is it in the interests of this country to continue to supply such grants when they serve to keep a regime in power which is patently bent on aiding the Soviet Union, whose avowed purpose is to do us in? I think not. Moreover, we need to enlist the support of friendly countries around the littoral, not alienate them.

Specifically, we should be exerting every effort to help Brazil, Argentina, and Venezuela to modernize their own naval forces. On the African side of the ocean we should judiciously combine diplomacy and economic aid in a carefully orchestrated program to move key nations to our side of the fence. Some military aid may be in order, despite the volatile nature of the region. By providing basic coastal defense navies to some of these countries, we could go far toward insulating them against subversive infiltration or overt assaults from the sea by their neighbors. Yet we would still leave control of the open ocean to those western and western-oriented nations possessing true blue-water fleets.

In brief, these are the initiatives the United States ought to be taking to blunt the current Soviet drive in this part of the world. Furthermore, since the pattern examined in the South Atlantic is similar to that obtaining in other parts of the world, I would submit that these same kinds of actions ought to apply elsewhere as well. At the moment, however, there is an obstacle of major proportions: the size of the U.S. Navy. At its lowest level in numbers of ships since the mid-1930s, the navy is not today capable of countering the Soviet worldwide maritime offensive. And it will be even less capable of doing so in the next decade or two unless its size and basic structure are substantially altered.

Exploiting American Strengths. As I indicated at the outset of this discussion, I believe our approach to the very real threat posed by the Soviet Union must utilize total force. Its underlying philosophy will have to focus on full exploitation of those areas where the United States still enjoys superiority over the Soviet Union. With respect to technology, for instance, we must maintain a strong research and development effort—in civil as well as military fields. Most especially, we must choke off the current spate of virtually indiscriminate exports to the Soviet Union and Warsaw Pact countries. The recent fight in Washington over the sale of the Cyber-76 computer system to the Soviet Union is a case in point. It is clearly not in our own national interest to sell to our antagonist advanced technology that he does not have, thus permitting him to devote his resources—which are finite, just as ours are—to other projects which may ultimately grant him the edge he needs to realize his fundamental objective: the demise of American power and the triumph of Soviet-led communism.

Industrial know-how falls into the same category as technology. These and the incredible productivity of U.S. agriculture are components of the total force we must apply to the Russian threat. To a degree, our actions will have to be reactionary inasmuch as Moscow has moved ahead of us in some areas; in those areas we will have to play catch-up ball. But we should not let this fact limit our effort. We must be innovative at the same time. As I noted earlier, innovation is not one of the Kremlin's strengths. While the Russian leaders are past-masters at the art of exploiting opportunities presented to them, they have demonstrated considerably less ability to create conditions which they can then use to further their international aims. We must, therefore, expend more effort on identifying those brewing international situations that might provide Moscow with new opportunities—and we must move to forestall Soviet gains. Only by employing total force in an enlightened manner can we ensure that Lenin's prediction will come true but that the democratic protagonist will triumph.

In summary, one must conclude that there *is* a global threat to the United States and the western way of life. Ill-perceived by its prospective victims, it is nonetheless real. We can take hope, however, in the fact that on numerous occasions the Kremlin has revealed that it is something less than infallible. Confronted with a threat of this nature, innovative American policies will surely emerge victorious in the end. But unless we move promptly and positively, we may lose the contest by default. The course we must chart, it seems to me, is manifest.

Strategic Deterrence and a Strong Navy. Of supreme importance, of course, is the maintenance of strategic deterrence. For this, it is essential that we redress the strategic nuclear imbalance at the earliest possible moment. If we are protected by the strategic nuclear umbrella, we can prevent coercion of ourselves and our friends, while at the same time taking whatever conventional measures will ensure our own success and halt the onrush of Soviet-led communism. The task, to be sure, will not be an easy one. Differing approaches to strategic nuclear war as elucidated by Richard Pipes, domestic spending pressures, and the refusal of American leaders to reveal unpalatable facts to our citizens are all formidable hurdles. Nonetheless, these factors are intimately related to our national survival.

Once strategic deterrence is assured, then what? I would reiterate that the growth in Soviet international outreach has paralleled the emergence of a comprehensive Soviet maritime capability. Our counter-action should, therefore, exploit the same arena. As an insular nation which has for two centuries excelled in this environment, the United States should concentrate on sea power as one of its comparative strengths. We should not limit ourselves to such action, but employ it as a part of the total force concept with all of the flexibility we can manage. Conversely, we will ignore the maritime arena at our extreme peril. The final question to be answered, therefore, is what kind of navy does the United States need to do this portion of the job?

In my considered, professional judgment, it must be a fleet which is affordable yet sufficiently large and powerful to confront successfully the Soviet Union's worldwide offensive. We must use our current advantage in aircraft carriers to the maximum extent so long as these ships have sea-going life remaining in them. Now, however—as a matter of immediate priority—we must begin to construct the fleet of the future. We cannot wait for a latter-day Pearl Harbor to demonstrate to us that a new naval age has dawned. We must, of course, disperse tactical aviation at sea on an optimum number of platforms. After all, a nuclear-engined aircraft carrier, powerful though it unquestionably is, can be in but one place at a time. If the vital action does not happen to be taking place there, that particular bird farm is something less than useful. Therefore, we must begin now to construct medium-sized (40–60 thousand tons), conventionally powered carriers to operate fixed-wing aircraft. These carriers (CVV) would cover the transition period until vertical/short take-off and landing (V/STOL) technology can be perfected. In the event it cannot, the CVV would provide an alternative, permitting us to maintain tactical aviation at sea into the foreseeable future. If, on the other hand, we do solve the not inconsiderable problems of V/STOL technology, the new aircraft could be sent to sea on existing CVVs and on smaller (20–35 thousand ton), cheaper, V/STOL carriers (VSS) in numbers adequate to meet our needs.

Further, we must press ahead with lower-cost (again, this means affordable in adequate numbers) missile-armed surface combatants capable of facing off with ships of the Soviet navy—and winning. These and other new types of ships should be designed to carry V/STOL aircraft where feasible, thus further dispersing our seaborne tactical aviation. To do all this, we will have to capitalize on one of our nation's greatest strengths: America's technological superiority over the Soviet Union. By these means we can develop and field new naval capabilities and employ new concepts which will allow us to negate the maritime gains made during the past twenty years by the Soviet navy under the astute leadership of Sergei Gorshkov.

The Importance of Will and Leadership. Finally, there is one ingredient without which the foregoing prescription will avail us little. We must have the national will and determination to run the course. Above all, this requires the understanding and backing of the American people. It has been my experience, as I have talked to Americans across the country, that if they are given the facts they will almost unanimously support whatever action may be necessary to solve the problem. As one looks back across the pages of history, it seems clear that, while the people have usually been willing to face the facts, their leaders have often been reluctant to reveal those facts to them. And, I might add, this reluctance usually stems primarily from political fears among the ruling elite.

Unless the American leadership—the President of the United States, the secretary of state, and the secretary of defense—stand up and say to the American people, "Ugly though they may be, these are the facts," the determination that will be required cannot materialize. In short, our elected leaders have simply got to level with those who put them in office. If they do, we shall eventually triumph; if they do not, we shall surely make self-fulfilling the prophecy of Henry Kissinger that the United States has passed its historic high point like so many earlier civilizations.

4

THOUGHTS ON OUR NATIONAL STRATEGY FOR THE FUTURE

Theodore R. Milton

The Role of Nuclear Forces

"We have lost our atomic monopoly. We are probably inferior to the U.S.S.R. in numbers of ballistic missiles. We have no anti-ballistic missiles. . . . We have made no realistic effort to cope with Communist strength on the ground." The words are those of General Maxwell Taylor, written eighteen years ago in *The Uncertain Trumpet*.[1] The world has gone around a good many times since then, but the statement is, if anything, more accurate today than when it was written.

Once again, we have no defense against ballistic missiles, and our short-lived anti-ballistic missile (ABM) program was probably the last of its kind for the foreseeable future. The Soviet Union certainly exceeds us in throw-weight, if not in numbers of missiles. As for General Taylor's last point, a realistic effort to cope with Soviet ground strength is as far off as ever. Taking the facts of life, both demographic and economic, into account, we must admit that the likelihood of our ever again raising an army much larger than the present one, with its total strength of 765,000 (as contrasted with 8,260,000 at the end of World War II), is remote indeed. It could only be done with peacetime conscription, and the all-volunteer force (AVF), for better or worse, is undoubtedly here to stay. However one views the AVF, one thing seems certain: the concept itself will inevitably limit the size of those forces even if we decide to buy larger forces. We will not, in short, be in a position to challenge the Soviet Union in any situation where sheer weight of numbers is a decisive factor. And since a conventional war always does hinge on numbers and attrition, I appear to have written off our nonnuclear forces as a factor in any

[1] *The Uncertain Trumpet* (New York: Harper and Brothers, 1959), p. 6.

U.S.-Soviet military confrontation. Well, not quite. An ability to face up to a nonnuclear conflict is essential to our survival, at least to our survival as a great power. The question is how to do it.

A few years before Maxwell Taylor's frustrations found their way onto the best-seller lists, U.S. military strategy was a thing of stark simplicity. The bomber, armed with a nuclear warhead, had become the ultimate weapon. Everything else, whether ground troops, ships, or tactical aircraft, rated a poor second in priority. In fact, the only sure way for these other forces to get any serious attention at all was to claim some SAC supporting role. A movie produced on contract for SAC for the edification of Rotary Clubs and other civic gatherings in the mid-1950s showed, in a wonderfully simplistic way, how a bomber or two made superfluous all the other expensive paraphernalia of war: the troops, the ships, the fighter planes, were all neatly crossed out. The strategic bomber, majestic and unopposed, would take care of things. Happily, the film was suppressed at birth by the Pentagon, never to entertain the civic groups. Nevertheless, it expressed a point of view widely held in that period.[2] It was a point of view that had been buttressed by the success of our confrontation with the Soviet Union over the blockade of Berlin in 1948–1949—the only armed confrontation between the two powers until that time.

The truth was that, faced with overwhelming Soviet ground and tactical air superiority, the U.S., British, and French occupation forces in Germany would not have been even a remotely credible adversary to the Soviet Union without the threat of nuclear weapons. The allied postwar demobilization had left nothing in reserve except the bombers of the Strategic Air Command. With only the threat of those B-29s, aided by the ominous deployment of a few of them to England, we were able to carry out the incredible, and from a military standpoint, preposterous, Berlin airlift. The peaceful resolution of the grave Berlin crisis depended on the airlift's success—which in turn depended on the ability of unarmed and unescorted transport airplanes to plow back and forth on a precise course and schedule, keeping inside ten-mile-wide air corridors. The Soviet Union had only to jam the navigation beacons and instrument landing systems—procedures which would have been child's play—to thoroughly disrupt the airlift. Presumably, the Soviet Union wanted victory in Berlin, yet it did nothing to interfere with the vulnerable operation that was denying them

[2] The author was one of a small group who reviewed this movie at the Pentagon. The secretary of the air force, the Honorable James H. Douglas, and the chief of staff, General Thomas D. White, decided against approval of this movie for public release. So far as I know, it disappeared without a trace.

victory. In the brief years of our nuclear supremacy we had a strategy that worked.

The Realities of "Flexible Response." The Berlin blockade was a clear warning of future Soviet intentions, and its aftermath saw the formation of NATO. Here again, the Strategic Air Command was the real foundation on which NATO was built. The original strategy of the alliance was primarily one of reliance on the United States's capacity for and, of equal importance, its commitment to massive retaliation in exchange for any Soviet incursion in Europe. Under this reassuring umbrella a thin line of ground troops in NATO would do, their purpose that of a burglar alarm or, as the strategists called it, a trip wire. To a very real extent, that philosophy, though no longer NATO's formal strategy, has persisted to this day. In 1967, after protracted wrangling, NATO adopted a strategy of flexible responses,[3] but there has never been any evidence that this alliance of free nations really sets much store by it. Serious adoption of this strategy would involve a greater raising of ground troops and greater budget outlays than any western nation seems able to contemplate. The reliance on U.S. strategic forces is still widely regarded within NATO as the saving feature of this flexible strategy.

In theory, that reliance is sound enough. The U.S. strategic arsenal remains formidable by any standard. If it lacks weapons as big as the largest Soviet ones, it excels in accuracy, diversity, and, in all probability, technology. There should be no doubt as to the reliability and professional capability of this force, its submarines, its bombers, or its land-based missiles. Once triggered, U.S. strategic forces would almost surely destroy the Soviet Union beyond any acceptable limit. The danger lies not in the inadequacy of U.S. strategic forces but in two other factors: the speed with which the nuclear threshold is crossed, and the willingness of a U.S. President, any President, to set the strategic machinery in motion.

In any situation short of an unmistakable Soviet nuclear attack on this nation itself, there will always be enormous and conflicting pressures on a President contemplating the use of nuclear weapons. The very nature of our election process and the traditional way a President surrounds himself with advisors guarantees a certain presidential distrust of what may appear to the Joint Chiefs as the obvious decision. In addition, there is the fact that no one has ever fought a

[3] Flexible response is known as MC 14/3, the MC standing for the NATO Military Committee. Adoption of this strategy was one of the reasons given by France for withdrawing from the NATO integrated military structure.

nuclear war. Our own venture into that realm was hardly full of risk. Harry Truman's decision was, compared to that facing any President now, an uncomplicated one. Japan, already beaten, was simply being given the *coup de grâce*, and there was no possibility of Japanese retaliation.

Nowadays, a President must consider what he is risking when he gives the irrevocable command to launch his missile force. It is this very risk that has remained a principal argument for the manned bomber. Launching bombers is not a final decision; it gives a President an extra option, a sort of crutch. It is a way of doing something in the face of a crisis without actually doing everything. But the more basic decision to dispatch the warheads to their targets is where the buck stops. Since preventive war has long been ruled out as unthinkable for this nation, the timing factor, the speed with which the nuclear threshold is crossed, takes on immense importance. The nuclear threshold is a kind of misty border, not easily perceived from an abstract viewpoint. The West Germans, for instance, are staunch supporters of nuclear weapons in NATO. They also realize that tactical nuclear weapons will explode on German soil. So far, no problem. It is only when people start getting specific about where and when these weapons might be used that a certain schizophrenia seems to develop in the German planners.

If we rule out the obvious case, the situation where the Soviet Union simply starts a war by a missile attack on the United States, we can agree that our nuclear threshold has not been crossed until our forces are clearly *in extremis*. The concept in NATO under the flexible response strategy is, of course, to fight conventionally until there is no other recourse save nuclear weapons. Some optimists think NATO could hold out for weeks with conventional arms. There are pessimists who give the conventional defenses only a few days. In either case, the implication is the same: NATO must, under Soviet attack, eventually resort to nuclear weapons. This is another way of saying the United States must resort to those weapons, for it is the United States that must make the real decision if it is to be made in time. While NATO's conventional forces fought their delaying action a President would have time to condition himself to that unprecedented decision.

It is, of course, a wholly unlikely scenario. Nothing could be more foolhardy, from the Soviet standpoint, than to start a war with the United States in such a fashion, and so, by a kind of convoluted logic, the concept of troops in Europe makes a great deal of sense. Granted the forces there are inadequate in number, poorly deployed, and from NATO's standpoint badly organized, these troops are still capable of denying the Soviet Union a European walkover; thus they stand as assurance that there would be a decent interval before the nuclear threshold was crossed, an interval during which a President could sort out his decision. It is a nice checkmate, but it will not do as a strategy in the world that lies ahead of us.

The Role of Limited War

Ambassador George Kennan, in his book *The Realities of American Foreign Policy*, made the intriguing observation "that the day of total war has passed."[4] It is a statement that is reminiscent of one I recall hearing Zbigniew Brzezinski make somewhere or other, to the effect that war had become too expensive for rich nations. Only poor countries could now afford to fight.

The trouble with both of these statements is that they disregard the likely basis for any new big war, a war involving the developed world. So long as petroleum remains an essential source of energy, the developed nations of the West must have access to the petroleum of the Middle East. The oil fields and the oil routes themselves are an ever more likely source of conflict as western dependence grows and the Soviet Union seeks to establish client states in strategic locations. The ocean beds, a promising source of petroleum, will add one more likely source of conflict. Meanwhile, our own national strategy, such as it is, remains a defensive one save where it is complicated by ethnic pressures and such mystic goals as human rights. If, as Admiral Alfred Thayer Mahan believed, national strategy should be founded on principles of national self-interest, there is something very wrong with ours, for our own self-interest does not seem to be a major consideration.

An objective look down the road toward the twenty-first century is apt to bring on a touch of nostalgia. In spite of a civil war, other wars, dust bowls, and a Great Depression, our first two hundred years were probably easier than the century ahead. We face the bleak prospect of a world with too many people and too few resources, a world where the pressures for the maintenance of living standards in the developed nations will be in direct competition with the pressures for survival elsewhere. It will be a world where power will count for a great deal, perhaps everything; only power can contribute to an orderly, if perhaps inequitable, distribution of goods that are in short supply. It will take power to see to it that the developing countries do not withhold essential raw materials as a means of political or eco-

[4] George Kennan, *The Realities of American Foreign Policy* (Princeton, N.J.: Princeton University Press, 1954), p. 80.

nomic blackmail. And only military power can ensure the safety of lines of communication.

American Attitudes toward the Use of Force. Our own brief history as the unquestioned world power has come to an end, and we may well be in a transitional stage even now. For while the United States and the Soviet Union are clearly the two dominant world forces, there are reasons to doubt the ability of the United States to maintain its share of world military eminence. There is, first of all, our seeming lack of commitment to our own national interest. Any sensible move in that direction, whether it be weapons for Egypt or any other Arab country, or military aid for Turkey, or even the contemplation of a base in South Africa, is met with determined and successful opposition. Obviously, national interest will have to give way to other interests in this era.

Then there is the matter of our own stabilizing population. However beneficial zero population growth may be from the standpoint of human welfare, it has been historically a bad omen for a nation with serious military pretensions. Large armies, plainly enough, can only be raised from large populations.[5] The fact that we could, from a demographic standpoint, have a considerably larger army than our present one is academic. There is no disposition in the United States toward any of the measures that would be necessary for a significantly larger standing military force. The pressures are, to state the obvious, in the other direction. It is a reasonable hypothesis that we will continue to spend in the future about what we are now spending on military preparedness. The question that cannot be so easily reduced to a hypothesis is, preparedness for what?

There is an argument being made—and it is strengthened by our disillusionment in Vietnam—that military power is a commodity which is fast losing its value. The argument is, in part, a moral one. Strong nations, in this egalitarian world, should no longer enforce their will on the weak, partly because war between the strong has become so destructive as to be self-defeating. Most of what strategy we have is devoted to proving this latter thesis. The Trident, our ICBM force, all our strategic weapons array are evidence of our belief, or at least our hope, that we can make a nuclear exchange with the Soviet Union such an illogical prospect as to prevent its ever happening. It just may be that we can, and that total war, as Kennan said, is a thing

[5] Robert Strausz-Hupé, writing in *The Balance of Tomorrow* (New York: Putnam, 1945), had an interesting and far-sighted observation on this subject, one that seems very apropos today: "A sudden preoccupation with population questions on the part of statesmen, scholars and publicists generally signals crisis" (p. 41).

of the past. But what of the other kind of war, where military power is used for specific and limited purposes?

Historically, it has been the accepted prerogative of strong nations to resort to military force when it was necessary to their aims to do so. In our own case we have only rarely taken on a military equal, although we have used military force as a diplomatic adjunct fairly steadily throughout our history. Tripoli, Spain, Mexico, and the Sioux come easily to mind. The arguments of the moralists notwithstanding, it seems clear that the future will be no different from the past. Military force will continue to be an adjunct to foreign policy. Whether or not the United States abides by the new strictures against the use of military power, the Soviet Union, along with its Cuban surrogates, is already blazing the trail. The question thus seems to be what, short of defending the homeland, is worth fighting for. Its corollary is the question of the means and the arrangements for doing that fighting.

If we were to behave as great powers have historically behaved, there would be little trouble in deciding when to use military force. We would use it whenever our interests were threatened and diplomacy had failed. Since our interests are ever more tied in with those of the rest of the world as our dependency on imports grows, we might thus expect some busy times ahead for the armed forces. The fact that we do not behave in the traditional manner complicates the business of our security in the decade or two ahead. Beyond that, we appear to have halted our progress toward an identity as Americans, an identity that clearly emerged in World War II. That war apparently ended the divisions between Americans—North-South divisions, ethnic divisions, and those, deeply rooted in bigotry and upbringing, between people of different religions. During World War II these special categories gave way to a larger feeling of Americanism. Southern Baptists, Jews, and Irish Catholics flew together, were shipmates, and fought on the Normandy beaches side by side. The American sense of national pride reached the level of chauvinism. Admittedly, the blacks were still largely excluded from this new found sense of camaraderie in World War II, yet the national mood, which touched them too, was one of national unity. The press in World War II was very much in tune with this national mood, a mood that seemed to signal the coming of age of the United States as a nation.

Thirty-two years later we are divided once again. A curious form of dual citizenship has now become a major factor in our political process. The United States cannot decide dispassionately, on the simple grounds of self-interest, what it should do in the Middle East or Africa or Cyprus. The American Jewish lobby, unabashedly putting the interests of Israel on a level with those of the United States, has a decisive voice in Middle East policy. The Greek lobby has clearly had a powerful influence on Turkish-American relations, and never mind the damage this has done to our position in the eastern Mediterranean. As for Africa, the simplistic and wholly irrational standard of skin color seems to be a major factor in determining our course there. Since Africa is destined to play a major role in our future, it is discouraging to see how thoroughly the emotional, if tenuous, ties of American blacks to that continent influence their contribution to our African policy. The quasi-dual citizens have thus injected a new and troublesome element into the business of determining how best to serve our national interests. It is a complication that Admiral Mahan did not envision.

Hence, the world that lies ahead of us is somewhat more complex than the world the Soviet Union will encounter, or at least it would appear to be. As we make our way toward the year 2000, we will have to contend not only with our own citizens' divided loyalties but also with the further distraction of our disengaged citizens, noisy and often articulate, who in the name of the environment seem to oppose modern progress in any form. In this respect, the Soviet Union is in an enviable position.

It may be that colonialism in the formal sense has passed into history; the governors-general, the pomp and circumstance associated with the great empires, have indeed gone. But colonialism in a new form persists and is growing. Colonialism as practiced by the Soviet Union substitutes native satraps for governors-general, Cuban surrogates and disciplined insurgents for a foreign legion or Indian Army, but it is colonialism nonetheless, and it is working against our national interest. A means of countering this Soviet colonialism would seem to be an essential goal. With the memory of Vietnam still fresh, if distorted, this will not be an easy goal to reach.

To go back to *The Uncertain Trumpet* and the Kennedy years, the strategy that developed out of a disenchantment with the all-or-nothing concept was a backlash strategy. It was a time for concentrating on basics, a time of Green Berets, old airplanes, and small gunboats. Jungle skills, desert skills, any sort of local know-how could be taught to the lad from Brooklyn, and the United States could thus come to the aid of those who resisted Soviet colonization. To a limited extent, it was not such a bad idea. Had we proceeded no farther than this concept, Vietnam would have gone under years ago, true enough, but much more quietly.

For one thing, the draft would not have played such a part in arousing American emotions. Vietnam would have remained a dimly perceived affair concerning only the professional military, and our failure there would have been a relatively small one, a learning experience for the continuing struggle. That Vietnam became, instead, a root cause of national dissidence is too tiresome a subject to pursue. We all have our explanations for what happened in the 1960s and they make for equally dreary reading. It is enough to acknowledge this great American failure and to know that its effect on American policy will apparently be lasting. It is a failure that sent the Green Berets and all the other contingents committed to counterinsurgency into eclipse. Vietnam left us essentially where we had been before it all began, dedicated to the defense of Central Europe, to massive retaliation against the Soviet Union if it attacks first, and to an aimless Pacific policy backed up, as befits such a policy, with forces plainly inadequate for any serious task. Meanwhile the threat to our lines of communication, especially that critical one from the Arab oil fields around the Cape of Good Hope, grows visibly.

Conflicting Pressures

Listen to Harold Brown, who has always seemed to dissociate himself from the hawks, speaking on July 29, 1977, to the Northern California World Affairs Council:

> Our principal long-term problem continues to be the Soviet Union. Whether we like it or not, the Soviet leadership seems intent on challenging us to a major military competition. To quote a friend and colleague—someone whose professional efforts over the past 15 years have been focused on arms control and who during most of that time has considered that U. S. actions were driving the competition—"The principal factor driving the arms race now is the Soviet military buildup, strategic and tactical."
>
> The most evident—and dangerous—features of this challenge arise from the steady annual increases (in real terms) in the Soviet defense budget, the build-up and improvement of Soviet strategic nuclear forces, the modernization of Soviet ground and tactical air forces in Eastern Europe, and the growing sophistication of Soviet naval forces, which include a gradually expanding capability to project military power at considerable distances from Russia itself.[6]

Brown might have added a few words on the growing dilemma that confronts him as secretary of defense, a dilemma caused by the

[6] See Department of Defense (Public Affairs) news release, no. 353–77, p. 2.

conflicting pressures of defense needs and of political and economic realities. In the face of this Soviet challenge the obvious response on our part is to meet the challenge. If, as many informed people believe, the challenge is destined sooner or later to take shape as a military confrontation, nothing could be more important to the citizens of this nation than to be certain we could stand up to the challenge. However, nothing is that simple in the United States, at least not any more, and so defense spending will continue to have a steady and determined opposition.

In all fairness to this opposition, it must be said that the military occasionally furnishes the ammunition for the attacks on the defense establishment. Service rivalries, while not so openly fratricidal as in the days of the navy-air force battle over the B-36, nevertheless still contribute to public confusion over what, and how much, is needed. With that confusion comes a certain cynicism—and diminished support for all defense needs. In addition there is the fact that military men, like dedicated professionals in any field, tend to become subjective about their specialties, and the result is an overall weakening of the case for the defense dollar. In this atmosphere it is very difficult, if not downright impossible, for any collective and objective judgment to emerge. Years ago we could afford this intramural sport on the debatable grounds that a little rivalry produced better results. In the years ahead we cannot, for even our best efforts will be hard put to cope with the Soviet challenge. Without belaboring the point, a few examples might serve a purpose.

The Case of Air Power. Douhet, Mitchell, and Seversky may have put the case a little too strongly,[7] but the fact remains that air power is, and will continue to be, an essential element in our survival strategy. The problem with air power is that it keeps getting subverted. Each of our services is guilty of this subversion, and to the extent that each

[7] In his *The Command of the Air*, published in 1921, Douhet, as the apostle of strategic bombing, disdained fighters. The bombers would always get through. It was a lesson we had to unlearn in World War II. Giulio Douhet, *The Command of the Air*, trans. by Sheila Fischer (Rome: Revista Aeronautica, 1958).

Brigadier General William Mitchell deliberately sought court-martial in order to draw attention to his views on air power, views which were widely divergent from the conventional military thinking of the early 1920s. Colonel Alfred F. Hurley, USAF, permanent professor of history at the Air Force Academy, has written a definitive biography of Mitchell, one of our most intriguing military personalities (Indiana University Press, Bloomington and London, 1975).

Alexander de Seversky was a colorful character who flew as a Russian naval aviator in World War I. He became an aircraft designer—the P-47 Thunderbolt of World War II grew out of his designs—and an air power advocate. His writings drew a great deal of attention to aviation in the years preceding World War II.

is successful, valuable resources are drained away. If our potential enemies were Hottentots, even countless millions of Hottentots equipped with cross-bows, we could experiment with various forms of air power and no harm done. Unhappily, we are not facing the Hottentots, although it is sometimes hard to believe in the light of some of our defense outlays.

From an airman's standpoint, the Viet Cong were the Hottentots. Any old airplane that could stagger into the air could fly over Viet Cong territory with impunity, barring the occasional lucky hit from small arms fire. This gave people ideas. We developed gun ships, armed helicopters for close support, and a variety of tactics suitable for a permissive environment. When we went north of the demilitarized zone, it became a different story. There we were faced with modern surface-to-air missiles, sophisticated radar, and Mig-21 fighters. Our best electro-counter measures were needed for penetration and survival. From an airman's point of view, to go a few miles north was to go from the stone age to the late twentieth century. Had our non-war-winning strategy permitted us an invasion of North Vietnam, our ground troops might have found, conversely, some satisfaction in facing a conventional, rather than a guerrilla, enemy.

The fact is that Vietnam, quite apart from the political and social trauma it caused, did nothing very instructive for us militarily, certainly not as much as it cost us. The army became over-dependent on air support, and air support of a kind highly vulnerable against a modern force. The air force, anxious to please the army and hold on to the mission of close support, developed the A-10, an aircraft of doubtful survivability in a modern conflict. The navy, cruising unmolested back and forth over its mounting coffee grounds at Yankee Station in the South China Sea, provided a convenient base for strikes against North Vietnam but not, considering all the land-based air forces available, an essential one. Aside from the fact that naval aviation proved its high degree of professionalism, Vietnam did nothing to clarify the future role of carrier-based aviation.

Europe. Our only clearly defined strategy remains the defense of Europe against a Soviet attack. Really, it is more a strategy of convincing the Soviet Union of the folly of such an attack. It is essentially the pre-World War II strategy of the British and French, complicated by the implied use, at some point, of nuclear weapons. It is not in any sense a war-winning strategy. There are no goals involved in this concept—unless yielding ground grudgingly can be called a goal—other than the wistful hope that it will prevent war.

Clearly we cannot abandon our European security pact. As the leader and principal bulwark of the Atlantic Alliance we cannot back away from those responsibilities. Nevertheless, we should remember that while we are the ally of our European partners, they are not, except in their own defense, necessarily ours. When our interests are threatened outside the narrow confines of the alliance, NATO is not engaged. The national interests of the individual NATO nations would come briskly forward if the United States alone were threatened, and the United States would be left to pursue its own ends without either commitment or, as in the case of the Yom Kippur War, even passive cooperation.[8] It seems clear, then, that we will need in the years ahead to come to some arrangements, and provide some forces, beyond those of NATO. Too much emphasis on European security is, like isolationism, a way of burying our heads in the sand.

Problems in the Postcolonial World. Professor Robert W. Tucker invented the phrase "forcible self-help" as a euphemism for armed intervention.[9] It is a phrase Mahan might have appreciated. At any rate, forcible self-help seems to be increasingly in evidence. We have the present struggle in the Horn of Africa and the recent, and probably future, clash between Egypt and Libya. Another outburst of forcible self-help appears inevitable between Israel and its Arab neighbors. The world, in short, is not through with the use of military power. The main difference between military power as a means of gaining an end in these times and military power used for the same purpose in the great days of the British Empire lies in technology. Lord Nelson could approach Trafalgar confidently in a fifty-year-old flagship. His edge lay in the quality of British ship handling and the courage of his men. A modern Nelson had better look to his radar and missiles, and so must the small nations who wish to fight other small nations. It is no good trying to go to war with F-84s against someone else's Mig-21s. Or with Mig-17s against F-4s.

Because armed conflict seems to be a very distinct possibility in so much of the emerging postcolonial world, the supply of modern weapons becomes of critical importance. From a moral standpoint, exporting modern armaments is probably questionable, especially to governments which are less than we would like them to be. But from the standpoint of our own national interest, and quite apart from any

[8] Portugal, several Portuguese governments ago, did let us refuel at Lages in the Azores, but our other allies were firmly uncooperative during the Yom Kippur War. It was an embarrassing moment for the alliance when national interests, namely fear of an Arab oil boycott, overshadowed the broader implications of the Middle East crisis.

[9] Robert W. Tucker, *The Inequality of Nations* (New York: Basic Books, 1977).

capitalist profit considerations, the sale of arms can lead to the most practical sort of alliances. Selling a modern weapons system to a client does not complete the transaction, it only begins it. The sale of an airplane, for instance, sets up a line of communication between this country and the client state for spare parts, training, the exchange of people back and forth, and even some sort of linguistic and cultural breakthrough. It sets the stage for mutual cooperation in matters where both of our interests are at stake, and also for mutual cooperation where only our own interests are involved. It is a way to gain at least limited basing rights, as the Soviet Union is currently demonstrating. And if we have sense enough, as we have had in the past, to behave responsibly and efficiently in the countries that buy our arms and seek our technical help, we will have created the basis for reliable alliances. In this connection, the concept of military assistance groups should be reviewed and perhaps rejuvenated. The work of such groups in the Philippines and Greece during their post-World War II insurrections could be a model for the days ahead. And it was military assistance that developed our close ties with Taiwan. Even if we no longer take seriously either the pretensions or the aspirations of the Nationalist Chinese, we must take seriously their merits, if we have any sense at all, for our own sake as well as theirs.

Our Military Force Needs. There remains, of course, the most difficult question, how to construct a U.S. military capability to deal with the world at large. Most of our sixteen army divisions are essentially equipped for and committed to Europe. Our tactical air forces are similarly committed, although there are some interesting possibilities here for diversion which we can contemplate in a moment. The marines, long associated with the Pacific, are being urged toward a new mission in NATO. And the navy, while still firmly part of whatever Pacific strategy we have left, finds itself tied, apparently inextricably, to the very doubtful maritime theater of the Mediterranean.

For reasons we discussed earlier, the prospects for raising any larger forces in this country appear dim. Our reserves are not only growing smaller with the disappearance of the draft, they are also, with the possible exception of the Air National Guard, growing more marginal in their potential usefulness. The problems associated with mobilization and readiness training make the immediate use of most of the reserves out of the question. The Air National Guard, because it has been modernized and because money and effort go into it, could substitute for the regular air force in a variety of situations, but it is the exception.

With our sixteen divisions, plus three relatively lightly equipped marine divisions, we are clearly not going to take on anybody, at least alone, in a large-scale ground war. Nor could we, with a tactical air force of seventy-four fighter/attack squadrons and no mass production of either airplanes or pilots to back them up, carry on an air war of attrition.

The answer to our dilemma seems to lie in making the most of what we are likely to have, which is to say roughly what we have now. This calls for a blurring, if not an actual elimination, of the traditional service roles and missions. There is, for example, nothing any longer uniquely naval about the sea. It is easily surveyed and reconnoitered these days by satellites. Ships at sea, anywhere at sea, can be found and attacked by long-range aircraft. Only the submarine can now view the sea as a haven. Thus, land-based air forces must enter into our naval strategy of the future. Unless the navy is to create a long-range land-based component, as the Soviet navy has done, the job becomes one for the air force. It would have been, in fact, an ideal mission for the B-1, an airplane whose demise we will increasingly regret.

Since it seems probable that the global interdependence our diplomats and economists now call the wave of the future will bring with it some global crises, there will be a need for an ability to get wherever the crises are. The tanker airplane would seem to be a key factor in this capability, along with some basing agreements.

It is curious that our development and exploitation of air-refueling has attracted so little attention, either among strategists or in the defense budget. It is a capability that enabled the United States during the Vietnam Tet crisis to fly a squadron of F-4s from South Carolina to Thailand and have them in combat forty-eight hours after the order came for their deployment. It was the capability that got a squadron of F-111s from Idaho to Korea within hours as a show of force following an incident in the Korean demilitarized zone. It is a capability that will need to be exploited in the years ahead. Tankers can, to some extent, make up for the absence of foreign bases, and tanker-supported aircraft can get anywhere in the world in hours, or at most a day or so.

Happily, air refueling is no longer just a tricky maneuver performed by bombers and fighters. Even the C-5A, our largest transport, can be air-refueled, and its crews are proficient in the tactic. This opens up the way for the air task force, tailored for whatever needs to be done. Here would be a new mission for the marines, who would appear to need a new mission as the likelihood of amphibious warfare grows remote. An air force/marine joint task force, with transports, reconnaissance, and air support, is something we could carry out. With the size of modern air transports, helicopters and even VTOL (vertical takeoff and landing) fighters could be brought along or, in the case of the VTOL fighters, air refueled.

Supplementary air support of naval forces could also be provided by tanker/fighter groups. And the tankers could enhance the versatility, staying power, and range of carrier aviation.

At the same time, the importance of the navy to our future security will grow. There is no substitute for a naval force in a situation where the presence of visible and lingering military power can be decisive. It would appear very much in our long-term interest to move toward a 600-ship navy, taking care meanwhile to see that the resulting fleet is designed to deal with its main adversary, an objective that has sometimes been lost sight of.

We must naturally continue to spend a substantial amount of our defense dollar on the ultimate weapons of strategic warfare. What is left is going to have to stretch. It must cover our NATO obligations, and they will be with us, we can hope, for a long time to come. It must also cover our nation's interests in a world where we are everywhere involved. We will be hard put to maintain forces the size of our present ones, let alone dream of any increase.

Because our main commitment, to NATO, is so essentially defensive, our residual capability and the strategy for its employment should have some preemptive elements. Admittedly, Vietnam was preemptive, and look where that left us. But the troubles ahead of us are not going to be solved if we remain afflicted by the Vietnam syndrome. We have the technology to produce superb precision munitions, which are great force multipliers: one plane armed with precision guided bombs can do the work of many armed only with ordinary iron bombs. And we have the technology to give us accurate, instantaneous intelligence. In our all-regular military services we also have a force ready to be dispatched anywhere without a mobilization buildup. If we combine this with a military assistance program to lay the groundwork for friendly deployment areas, we should be able to cope.

5

STRATEGIC GUIDELINES FOR THE UNITED STATES IN THE 1980s

Bruce Palmer, Jr.

The term "strategy," derived from the ancient Greek, originally pertained to the art of generalship or high command. In modern times, "grand strategy" has come into use to describe the overall defense plans of a nation or coalition of nations. Since the mid-twentieth century, "national strategy" has attained wide usage, meaning the coordinated employment of the total resources of a nation to achieve its national objectives.

Historical experience suggests that for a strategy to be successfully carried out, all actions and policies must be subordinated to the political objectives. Another hard lesson of history is that the military and economic means employed must be compatible with and adequate to fulfill the nation's political ends. A classic example of the failure to balance means and ends is the case of Japan in World War II. Not only were the Japanese vastly overextended in territory and manpower, but they went to war badly outmatched in terms of the economic-industrial base required to support modern warfare. Our own recent painful experience should remind Americans that a viable strategy must also have the support of the public and the political leaders at home.

From National Interests to Grand Strategy

National strategy is not developed in a vacuum but is shaped and guided by the national interests, objectives, and policies of the nation as articulated by its leaders. Theoretically, the genesis of all strategic planning is "the national interest"—the highly generalized concept of a nation's most vital needs. It is fair to say that every country has an abiding interest in its own security and well-being, which include the preservation of the existing political order. Thus the security of the nation implies more than protecting its citizens and defending its territory; it also requires maintaining the government's authority within its own borders and improving its position in the international order. Aristotle and Plato both expounded on the duty of the state to survive internal challenges as well as external threats from neighboring states, and so did our own founding fathers.

The national interest has been redefined over the years as the specific requirements of security and well-being became better understood. In the case of the United States, it was in the national interest in our early years—indeed it was our "manifest destiny"—to expand our territory from ocean to ocean; to fight a savage civil war, the first so-called total war in our experience, in order to preserve the Union; and to experiment with our own version of an overseas empire at the turn of the century. The Monroe Doctrine, enunciated in 1823, and a century later the acquisition of the Canal Zone in the new country of Panama fell within the prevailing interpretations of the national interest.

Matured by 200 turbulent years that have brought it superpower status, the United States has begun its third century uncertain as to its future role in the world. One might fairly ask, How do our people interpret the national interest today? Have the values we hold as a people changed in any fundamental way? Many cultures and subcultures exist within our society and a substantial proportion of our people, particularly our youth, do not share the values of older generations. Fortunately, many of our young people, as they mature, discover that they share the older values after all. It is equally apparent that among our 216 million people there remain many large, diversified minority and ethnic groups who perhaps have only one thing in common—they are American citizens.

Nevertheless, a substantial majority of our citizens of all ages still believe in the United States and the aspirations of the American people to shape a better world. If the American dream of creative ideas in an idealistic world yet breathes, who should doubt our ability to interpret our national interests in a way that will continue to preserve our way of life and our aspirations for a more perfect world?

The Need for a National Strategy. Some Americans today decry the apparent lack of a cohesive national strategy for the United States. After a humiliating defeat in Southeast Asia, the trauma of seeing a President compelled to resign to avoid impeachment or worse, and the unprecedented assumption of power by a nonelected President, our country is going through a period of reflection and retrospection. It is time to check the cut of our sails and set a new course for the ship of state—that is, if we assume that some expression of national direction, or national strategy, is desirable, guiding our people and clarifying our international role for friends and foes alike. But in fact, have we ever had a clear, cohesive statement of national policy?

The answer is probably no, although over the last three decades successive administrations have tried to articulate a coherent national policy: the Truman Doctrine spelled out the policy of containment and recognized the cold war as a state of affairs; President Eisenhower extended that policy with the emphasis on massive retaliation; the Kennedy-Johnson forward strategy recognized the nuclear standoff between the United States and the Soviet Union and stressed nonnuclear means to revitalize the concept of containment; and more recently the Nixon Doctrine, carried forward by President Ford, called for partnership with friends and allies and negotiations with potential opponents.

Only recently have the broad outlines of the national security policy of the new administration begun to emerge. The indications are that the policy of the Ford administration has not been substantially altered. The Carter strategy apparently seeks to counterbalance Soviet nuclear and conventional forces and at the same time to promote economic and political cooperation with the Soviet Union. The administration has also announced its intention to pay relatively more attention to the problems of Third World nations and less to bilateral relations with the Soviet Union.[1]

Although a detailed national plan of action may be neither feasible nor desirable, it should be possible to develop a strategic concept with a specific thrust. To be useful, such a concept must be flexible and versatile in order to meet unexpected developments that are bound to arise. This paper will attempt to set out the broad outlines of a strategic approach to the next decade for the United States.

Potential Sources of Conflict. Military strategic planners traditionally have gone about their business by first considering the so-called threat—that is, the various nations or possible coalitions of nations posing the greatest danger to the welfare and survival of the United States. The ultimate threat, of course, would be a military one threatening our very survival, but short of that there are many shades of potential economic, political, and military threat to the United States.

---

[1] Charles Mohr, "Carter Orders Steps to Increase Ability to Meet War Threats—Secret Directive on Strategy," *New York Times*, August 26, 1977; Zbigniew Brzezinski, "U.S. Policy in an Awakened, Complex World," *Washington Post*, November 1, 1977.

Let us, then, start with an evaluation of the potentially hostile elements in the world around us, since those clearly must be considered somewhere in the discussion.

The overall threat to the United States is a multidimensional one involving friends and allies as well as potential enemies. In a world where national economies are interdependent and the global economy extraordinarily dynamic, any stable global balance of power is unworkable as the basis of a national strategy. Even a limited political and military balance of power may not be feasible in a world community of almost 150 nations, some of which are extremely wealthy and many of which are relatively well armed. Multinational corporations wielding supranational power add another complex dimension. The North-South confrontation between the advanced nations and the Third World likewise cuts across traditional international alignments. Finally, it is clear that world population pressures and competition for scarce resources have already caused friction not just between "have" and "have not" countries, but also between friendly nations in both categories.

The greatest military threat to the United States is, of course, the Soviet Union, the other nuclear superpower. This basic fact, which is not expected to change over the next decade, is central to any strategy adopted by the United States. The presence and the nature of the constantly shifting multidimensional threat mentioned earlier does not and cannot alter this basic reality of power. Although there are other world power centers (Western Europe, Japan, the People's Republic of China [PRC]), and others may begin to emerge by the end of the 1980s (Brazil, India, Indonesia), the truth remains that in the stark terms of raw power, this still is a bipolar world dominated by the United States and the Soviet Union and will continue to be so over the next decade.

It is difficult to divine the intentions of the Soviet Union and unwise to try; nevertheless one can gain some insight from examining the Soviet Union's military capabilities and actions. Since the Soviet Union is building and maintaining forces to levels which appear to be well beyond those estimated to be required simply to defend the motherland and the parts of Europe and Asia that are under Soviet hegemony, it can be inferred that the Soviet Union is interested in expanding its influence beyond its present borders. Soviet meddling in areas far removed from the homeland supports this conclusion.

In the area of nuclear weapons, the Soviet Union has reached general parity with the United States. It would probably like to gain political and psychological advantage by building its arsenal to the point where, in both offensive and defensive weapons, it was perceived by the rest of the world as superior to the United States. Whereas the United States might refrain from using such an advantage except for deterrence, the Soviet Union probably would not hesitate to use it aggressively.

The existence of nuclear forces of awesome power tends to act as a brake on the level of any violence that otherwise might occur directly involving the superpowers. This is true, however, only if a mutual state of deterrence is maintained between them. It therefore appears to be in the interest of the United States to avoid a strategic arms race with the Soviet Union and to maintain a stabilized state of mutual deterrence, preferably at levels lower than those currently in effect. As added insurance, the United States must continue to rely on technological superiority in both offensive and defensive systems.

Since it is in the interest of both the United States and the Soviet Union to avoid fighting a nuclear war, nonnuclear conventional forces assume great importance as the only forces actually usable. In this light, the increasing emphasis placed by the Soviet Union on conventional military forces of all kinds poses an unpleasant prospect for the United States and its allies. Moreover, the absence of effective efforts to control conventional arms does not help the situation. Again, maintaining American qualitative superiority in both nonnuclear technology and trained military manpower is highly pertinent.

The People's Republic of China does not now, nor will it in the next decade, pose a major direct threat to the United States. If the Korean War can be considered to have been an aberration, the Chinese historically have tended to be friendly toward the United States. The People's Republic and the Soviet Union, on the other hand, historically have been hostile, and despite their common ideological allegiance, they now regard each other with distrust and suspicion. No doubt much of the current Soviet military buildup is designed to deal with the "Chinese problem." Similarly, the Soviet desire for détente with the West may be at least partially motivated by the dual objectives of (1) freeing the Soviet Union to focus its attention on China, and (2) undermining NATO.

Europe, yearning for genuine détente, uneasy over the possibility of Soviet nuclear superiority to the United States, and questioning its own ability to face the Soviet conventional-force buildup, is obviously hypersensitive to Soviet moves. The Soviet Union seems to understand this situation and has refrained in recent years from putting any direct overt pressure on West Berlin or Western Europe.

Military Strategy and Power. Within the broader framework of a national strategy, military strategy concerns the location, posture, and maneuver of military forces to support national political aims. National strategy involves both the threat of force and the use of force. It is immensely complicated when there exists a mutual threat of force of significant capability on both sides, thus increasing the importance of the military dimension compared with the purely political and economic dimensions of the rivalry between nations. *The essence of strategy is to neutralize or overcome the military threat, and at the same time establish the foundations for a political solution consonant with national political objectives.*

The paradox of military power (and this was becoming apparent in World War I, decades before the detonation of the first atomic weapon) has been the fact that the increasing efficiency and destructiveness of weapons systems make them increasingly difficult to control and thus increasingly less useful as instruments of policy, particularly in disputes between equally industrialized states. With the development of nuclear weapons and now a state of approximate equivalence between the two nuclear superpowers, we have mutual deterrence through the distinct possibility of mutual destruction. Although this balance of terror may not work, it nevertheless is the cornerstone of current U.S. deterrence strategy.

Mutual deterrence places the paradox of power in a new perspective, as nuclear power exists only in its capacity to destroy—if it is used, mutual destruction is the result. Moreover, the nature of nuclear power is such that no human brain can visualize the consequences of human and material devastation—inflicted with a speed and on a scale never before remotely experienced—that nuclear war would bring.

All strategic planners appear to agree that maintaining mutual strategic nuclear deterrence between the United States and the Soviet Union must have the highest priority in our defense establishment. The United States should also consider damage-limiting measures, although protecting our retaliatory capability must take precedence, and should eschew any special offensive nuclear options which might destabilize the balance of deterrence. The notion that defensive measures are inherently destabilizing has caused the defensive side of the strategic nuclear equation to be relatively neglected by the United States. Thus, a prudent offensive-defensive posture, in consonance with current strategic arms limitations, should be a top-priority goal of the United States.

With this kind of policy, we should have little fear that the Soviet Union might launch a first strike against the United States. Historically, the Soviet Union has been cautious in its foreign policy, reluctant to go to the brink of nuclear war and unwilling to endanger the homeland. During the nineteenth and twentieth centuries up until World War II, Russia, and then the Soviet Union, was the victim of aggressors from Europe and the Far East. Since World War II, the Soviet Union has established hegemony over Eastern Europe, crushing several revolts, and its proxies have invaded South Korea and overrun South Vietnam. The Soviet Union has fostered revolution and subversion in every continent on earth and in this sense has thwarted U.S. and allied forces deployed in a containment posture. But the fact remains that except in Eastern Europe, which it considers vital to the defense of the homeland, the Soviet Union has not committed its own forces to any significant degree outside its borders. This not only speaks well for our containment strategy, at least up to the present, but also is a strong indication that the Soviet Union will not risk committing any Soviet forces outside its present area of hegemony when to do so would place the motherland in jeopardy.

As we have seen, conventional military power is the only usable force available. Moreover—and it is the great novelty of the present situation—modern, sophisticated conventional arms and trained foreign military advisors are widely available in ever increasing numbers all over the globe. Practically any small country can now start a fair-sized war, and the only real means of control available to the powers for whom these small countries are proxies is the resupply or withholding of ammunition, fuel, spare parts, and so on, the sinews of modern warfare. This is a development of profound significance because it reduces the military power gap between the large industrial powers and the less developed powers. This exacerbates the paradox of military power, for it further limits the effectiveness and usefulness of military force.

A Geopolitical Look at the United States and Its Interests

Before designing a national strategy, we should take a look at our geopolitical position: Just what kind of a nation is the United States? We are at the same time both an insular country and a continental one. First, two great oceans wash our flanks. In national security terms, these great waterways offer some degree of protection from enemies off the continent (though far less than they once did), but they also provide routes of attack and invasion, on and below the surface. They are the unequalled carriers of international trade as well as of domestic traffic, provided that we have free access to them. And below these immense waters lies untold wealth in minerals and other natural resources of which the nations are becoming acutely aware. Although the Bering Strait, separating the state of Alaska from the Soviet Union, is only a few miles wide, there are no land bridges to the North American continent. As for the air space above us, it, too, offers routes of attack and invasion, in particular aerospace attack over the north polar region; yet the air is also a major medium of transportation, almost monopolizing the intercontinental transport of people and carrying a relatively small but vital part of foreign and domestic trade, namely high-value items demanding high-speed transport. But in terms of defense, ballistic missiles, land and sea-based, have permanently destroyed our air and sea barriers. Now our insular position no longer protects us and we are no less vulnerable than a continental nation with enemies on its land borders.

The United States, of course, is also a continental nation. It has been dominant in North America since the mid-nineteenth century when its territory first extended from the Atlantic to the Pacific and it acquired most of the inhabitable temperate zone of the continent. Although our country's large land mass allows considerable dispersion of industries and critical defense installations, there are areas in the United States of high industrial and population density, such as the Northeast, which are highly vulnerable to aerospace attack.

In the past, our political, economic, and social development as a nation has been fortuitously blessed. For most of our first 200 years, our contiguous oceans acted as immense moats and we enjoyed the protection of friendly foreign fleets, in particular the British fleet. Although we rose to world prominence as a major sea power after the Spanish-American War, it was not until World War II that the decline of the British Royal Navy sank home and the United States realized that henceforth it would have to guard its own sea frontiers and assume the burden of maintaining the Anglo-American tradition of freedom of the seas. Air power came of age in World War II, and since that time the United States has been the foremost air and sea power in the world, unchallenged until very recently.

We were fortunate in our land position, too. Canada and the United States have been traditionally friendly and continue to enjoy the longest unfortified international border in the world. Our relations with our other neighbor, Mexico, have been stormy in the past and we stationed troops along the Mexican border up until Pearl Harbor when we entered World War II. But Mexico has never been a threat, only a source of possible harassment.

Thus, historically, the United States has had no need to maintain forces for the defense of its continental land borders. This is not to say that the United States is not a land power, however. Our Civil War was fought primarily on land and on a grand scale, the largest land war ever fought up to that time and the first total war in modern times. (Sea power played a key role, too, in helping the Union to deny the South economic and diplomatic aid from outside sources and to split the Confederacy by seizing control of the Mississippi River.) In World War I, American land power, transported and sustained by sea power, stemmed the tide in Europe and helped our Allies defeat the Central Powers. And again in World War II, U.S. land power, working in close coordination with U.S. air and sea power and in harmony with our Allies, helped defeat the Axis powers in both Europe and the Pacific. In short, even though it may not consider itself to be a land power, a nation of 216 million people dominating one of the major choice land masses of the globe and possessing great human talents and material resources must be accepted as a land power.

Today, however, the United States should be considered a strong military power all around—not just a sea, air, or land power. Modern warfare has taught us that no one service can go it alone, but that each needs the others in one way or another. Moreover, a synergistic effect is generated by the proper, mutually reinforcing employment of the forces of all the services. Thus, our defense doctrine stresses balanced U.S. forces, strategic and conventional, of all services, avoiding any undue reliance on any one service, weapons system, or military strategy. History tells us that this is the only prudent approach since no one has ever accurately foretold the nature of a conflict. All we know for sure is that the nature of future warfare is uncertain and that the consequences of guessing wrong could be catastrophic for our survival.

What will our geopolitical position be in the world of the 1980s? Starting with the United States and North America, let us take a look at various regions of significant interest to the United States.

The United States and the Western Hemisphere. At home, the state of the economy and the social health of the nation will be the paramount factors affecting our national security posture. Prolonged economic stagnation with attendant chronic high unemployment would have a pervasive, dampening effect on our whole society. How much success we achieve in solving our urban ills is even more critical to the nature of our national outlook over the next decade. Our present record is not impressive and the possibility of major unrest, dissatisfaction, and civil discord in the future cannot be ignored. If such developments occur, they obviously will have serious adverse implications for our police forces at home, as well as for our ability to deal with international crises.

Our immediate neighbors may also pose more complex problems in the future. Separatist movements in Canada could quite possibly involve the United States. And possible political and economic instability in Mexico and an exploding population will bring increasing pressure on our southern border as more and more Mexican citizens push north seeking a better homeland.

We must keep in mind that the Western Hemisphere as a whole constitutes the base area of the United States and as such is of fundamental importance to our security.

(1) Canada, occupying a strategic area to our north, is uniquely important to the security of the United States since the two nations would be equally endangered by an intercontinental aerospace attack on either one. Thus, there is good reason for close cooperation between the two countries on defense matters of the kind exemplified by the North American Air Defense Command (NORAD).

(2) The Caribbean Sea region has traditionally been of strategic importance to the United States. Like the Gulf of Mexico, the Caribbean is too close to home and crossed by too many heavily traveled trade routes of great value to the United States to allow it to become dominated by any major foreign power. The Caribbean region has generally been described as encompassing Cuba and the other islands of the West Indies, the eastern littoral of Central America, the Panama Canal area, and the northern littoral of South America, specifically Colombia and Venezuela. The Caribbean lies astride the sea approaches to the Gulf of Mexico and to the eastern end of the Panama Canal. The canal is economically important to the United States and its Latin American neighbors, and in fact constitutes the economic lifeline of the countries on the western coast of South America. The canal is also of major defense interest to the United States since it would allow the passage of warships and military cargo and would serve as a base in time of war.

(3) American "sovereignty" in the Canal Zone has been a bone of contention not only with Panama, but also with all other members of the Organization of American States (OAS). For this reason, the U.S. government has sought to renegotiate the status of the zone on a basis more acceptable to Panama and other Latin American countries, yet still guaranteeing the security and neutrality of the canal as an international waterway and safeguarding against its falling under the control of a hostile regime. Provided these guarantees are met, a new agreement is considered to be in the best interests of the United States. The newly negotiated treaties, if and when ratified by the U.S. Senate, call for the removal of U.S. forces by the year 2000. In this long-term time frame, consideration should be given to the use of an

international OAS force, including U.S. and Panamanian contingents, to safeguard the neutrality of the canal.

(4) South America as a whole is a significant asset to the United States. Not only is there the major trade that flows between North and South America, but there are natural resources in the southern latitudes that are of strategic value to the United States. Today, the United States must import oil and some eighteen other strategic materials—resources required not just for munitions but for U.S. industry. More than half of these critical materials are found in South America, and all but two are located in the Western Hemisphere.[2] This U.S. dependence will increase with time as competition for scarce resources expands.

(5) Politically and economically, many Latin American countries can be characterized as nations of extremes. This, coupled with traditions of political revolution, has led to the establishment of numerous authoritarian regimes, some civilian and some military, usually dedicated to economic betterment and social reform without recourse to the alternative of communism. Many of these governments are considerably further to the left or right of center than is comfortable for the United States. This is a fact of life that we must understand and accept if we as "Norte Americanos" are going to live in harmony with our Latin American friends.

(6) Brazil is the gargantua of South America, dwarfing in territory and population all other South American states. It has borders with every other country in South America except Chile and Ecuador, and it has all the prerequisites for becoming a new world power center—a large population (about 110 million), talent, a strong cultural heritage, abundant natural resources, and a strategic geographic position. More important, its present leaders deeply believe in a "manifest destiny" that will make Brazil the dominant power in South America and in the South Atlantic. Brazil occupies a strategic position in the South Atlantic and could become the site of valuable military bases. Its essentially military-controlled government espouses a geopolitical doctrine that divides responsibility for policing the hemisphere between Brazil and the United States. The Brazilians are well on their way to fulfilling their aspirations and by the end of the 1980s could emerge as a world power center.[3]

In terms of their relative capability to employ conventional military power in the Western Hemisphere, the Soviet Union simply

[2] "U.S. Defense Needs—A Look Ahead," Association of the U.S. Army (AUSA) Paper, November 9, 1976, pp. 3–4.

[3] Penny Lernoux, "Brazil's Drive to Its Destiny," *Washington Post*, June 9, 1977.

cannot compete with the United States. This was dramatically demonstrated during the Cuban missile crisis of October 1962 when Khrushchev recognized that Cuba was beyond the range of Soviet conventional forces and retreated from his exposed position in the Caribbean Sea literally under the American guns. Perhaps of greater significance is the obvious fact that whereas the area is of vital importance to the United States, it is not to the Soviet Union. Thus, in this instance, the balance of perceived national interest as well as the balance of military power is strongly against the Soviet Union.

From this brief discussion one could reasonably conclude that in its own self-interest the United States should nourish and maintain, for the foreseeable future, a special relationship with Latin America in general and with Canada, Brazil, Mexico, and Panama in particular.

Europe. Turning to the continent of Europe, the United States regards Western Europe (including the United Kingdom) as vital to the overall security of the nation. The assumption that the loss of Europe to an unfriendly power or coalition would irretrievably turn the scales against the United States has been one of the basic tenets of our national strategy throughout the twentieth century. In World War I, we sent our forces across the Atlantic to fight on the side of the Allied Powers, and in World War II, the Allied strategy was to concentrate on the defeat of Germany first, before shifting the weight of our effort against Japan. Our steadfast support of NATO today attests to this unchanging strategic decision.

Will this assumption continue to stand up during the 1980s? Is it based just on sentimental ties with the "old country" from which sprang much of our heritage and cultural traditions? The answer to the first question is yes, to the second, no. Our bond with Europe is not flimsy or passing. The human talent, creativity and culture, manpower, technology, and industrial capacity of the region surely make it unique in the world. In 1975, an analysis of the relative shares of world industrial output gave the Soviet Union and Eastern Europe 34 percent; the United States and Canada, 25 percent; Western Europe, 23 percent; Asia, 10 percent; and Latin America and all others 8 percent.[4] It is true that Western Europe is plagued with economic problems and political instability and that the growing strength of Eurocommunism is worrisome (though it is a double-edged sword for the Soviet Union). And no doubt Asia and Latin America will claim considerably larger shares of the world's industrial output by the end of the 1980s. Moreover, the notion of maintaining, through the manip-

[4] "U.S. Defense Needs," AUSA Paper, p. 5 (data from *Fortune* magazine).

ulation of power and diplomacy, a global balance among a world community of almost 150 nations, each with a mind of its own and even some local military clout, seems no longer feasible. Rather, as one prominent political scientist has put it, we must learn to live in a dynamic world of "international indeterminacy."[5] Nevertheless, one must conclude that (1) Western Europe clearly has the capacity to remain one of the world's truly great power centers, and (2) the loss of the area in the foreseeable future would be a stunning psychological, political, economic, and military blow to the power and prestige of the United States.

Geographically, Western Europe is defensible. Although it encompasses several major industrial states, Europe is in reality a peninsula jutting out from the Asiatic mainland rather than a bona fide continent. Indeed, Western Europe is only the western end of the peninsula. Its defense would involve a relatively short ground front whose flanks and rear would rest on sea frontiers which NATO forces should be able to control. The central region lacks territorial depth and the air battle would be especially crucial to the defense of rear areas which are crowded with air and naval bases, logistical installations, and other military facilities, but which are relatively weak in air defenses. Even so, NATO forces should be able to prevail.

On the southern flank, Italy, Greece, and Turkey all admittedly have internal political and economic problems of considerable dimensions, but their allegiance to NATO should survive for the foreseeable future. Their terrain and geographical location would make them difficult to invade. In addition, Yugoslavia would in all probability not only resist any violation of its territory by the Warsaw Pact, but also take unkindly any Warsaw Pact incursions into Italy or Greece. Historically, the Balkans have been best left alone by outsiders, as Germany in World War II was the last to discover. Turkish animosity towards the Soviet Union runs deep and the Turks can be expected to fight well in defense of their homeland. The eastern Mediterranean might prove to be a difficult area for the U.S. Sixth Fleet if hostilities were to break out, but certainly the central and western Mediterranean including the Strait of Gibraltar "belong" to NATO air and naval forces, which should be able to maintain control of the region. Spain, occupying a strategic position at the tip of the European peninsula, adjacent to the NATO base in the Crown Colony of Gibraltar, is eager to be associated with NATO. Spain should become

[5] Robert J. Pranger, *Defense Implications of International Indeterminacy* (Washington, D.C.: American Enterprise Institute, 1972).

more and more an asset to the West in the future, and we should encourage our NATO allies to accept it.

Today, "Middle Europe," the pivotal area, is permanently split, with the Federal Republic of Germany a member of NATO and East Germany a member of the Warsaw Pact. In this respect, the interests of both sides coincide: neither wants to see a reunited Germany occupying the pivotal area again. This curious paradox probably acts as another brake on actual hostilities in the region.

NATO strategy is one of deterrence, ultimately resting on U.S. strategic nuclear power, and its current basis is the assumption that the NATO allies can muster sufficient conventional defenses (1) to make the Soviet Union think twice before launching a conventional attack, (2) to raise the nuclear threshold to a less dangerous level, and (3) to allow the political heads of both sides, if conflict should nevertheless break out, time and opportunity to consider the consequences of escalation. Tactical (theater) nuclear weapons are an important link in the total spectrum of deterrence, but there is no evidence to suggest that it would be advantageous for the United States and NATO to initiate theater nuclear warfare. In other words, tactical nuclear weapons cannot substitute for adequate conventional forces.

Some are pessimistic about NATO's defenses in the face of a continued Soviet military buildup, conventional and nuclear. But there are several reasons for more optimism. A basic one is the questionable reliability of the East European contingents in the Warsaw Pact. The twenty-seven Soviet divisions now stationed in Eastern Europe[6] obviously pose a constant threat to NATO and indicate a strong Soviet intention to defend the area, but they are also there to preserve the status quo in a divided Germany and to assure the continued subordination of the East European satellites to the Soviet Union. Some go so far as to argue that the Soviet Union undertook a military buildup in the Warsaw Pact countries for internal reasons—to increase the strain on the East European economies, thereby slowing down any liberalizing tendencies in those countries, and to help the Soviet arms industry, which has been losing some clients.[7]

There are other complex factors affecting the relative strength of the opposing forces—for example, the heavy diversion of Soviet forces to the Chinese border and the growing influence of Eurocommunism in NATO countries. However, there are no basic reasons why the

[6] John M. Collins, "American and Soviet Armed Services, Strengths Compared, 1970–1976," *Congressional Record*, Senate, No. 135, Part III, p. S14097.

[7] Michael Getler, "Goulash Communism Savored," *Washington Post*, September 14, 1977.

United States and its NATO allies cannot provide enough forces to assure a credible, viable deterrent. Manpower, materiel, and money will be there if the will is manifest. Finally, the perceived balance of national interest is against the Soviet Union, since the United States has a far greater stake in Western Europe than does the Soviet Union.

The credibility of the U.S. contribution to this defense rests, at least in part, on our ability to mobilize backup forces, provide the necessary manpower and resupply to sustain our forces in combat, and protect our sea and air lifelines across the North Atlantic. Overemphasis on our part on the hypothesis that any conflict would be of short duration could lead to miscalculation on the part of the Soviet Union. On the other hand, a visible, credible American ability to mobilize for a longer haul is an important element of deterrence.

Inherent in this declared capacity to fight a long war if necessary is a credible capability to protect the sea lanes. Soviet naval forces, with unprecedented numbers of submarines, could effectively deny free access to the high seas if the U.S. Navy and allied fleets did not concentrate their attention on sea lines of communication (LOCs). In short, the Soviet Union must be made to perceive that it cannot win a long war.[8]

Although the Soviet Union enjoys an all-land LOC much shorter than our trans-oceanic LOC for the support of its forward deployed forces, it has compensating vulnerabilities. Its land LOCs are a long way from the western Soviet Union and pass through satellite nations whose dedication and reliability in all probability will not match the Soviet Union's. Allied air interdiction of these LOCs should play a major role in blunting any Warsaw Pact offensive. Soviet naval forces, split by geographical necessity into widely separated fleets, operate at a basic disadvantage. NATO's naval forces have the advantage of dominating geographic choke points, such as the Turkish Straits and the Baltic bottlenecks, to help them confine Soviet naval forces in the Baltic and Black Seas to their home waters. Moreover, since the Soviet Union's main naval forces are based far north in the Barents Sea, NATO forces plugging the Greenland-Iceland-Faeroe gaps would seriously hinder egress by Soviet ships into the North Atlantic as well as their return to home bases.[9]

In summary, the defense of Europe remains second in importance only to the defense of the United States and its essential base and water areas in the Western Hemisphere. Defense by the NATO allies

[8] Admiral Isaac C. Kidd, Jr., USN, "NATO Strategic Mobility," proceedings of the 1977 Worldwide Strategic Mobility Conference, National Defense University, Fort McNair, Washington, D.C., May 2, 1977, p. II–C–3.

[9] Ibid.

is feasible and reasonably attainable from a resource point of view over the next decade, but the United States and its allies must believe in that defense and accord it the priority it deserves.

The Middle East. For this discussion, the Middle East is defined as encompassing: the eastern Mediterranean and its coastal states, Libya, Egypt, the Red Sea and the states on both coasts, the Horn of Africa, the Arabian Peninsula, the Persian Gulf area, Iraq and Iran, the Gulf of Oman, and the Arabian Sea. This is one of the most strategic areas in the world, not only because of the vast amounts of oil found in the region, particularly in the basin of the Persian Gulf, but also because of its geopolitical position. Major world air and sea routes transit the area, which also constitutes a land bridge between the Eurasian land mass and the continent of Africa. And the Middle East is of great cultural, historical, and religious significance. It was the birthplace of western civilization and contains Jerusalem and Mecca, the symbolic centers of three great religions, Christianity, Judaism, and Islam. As an energy source the area is vital to most of the industrialized powers of the world today and crucial to the aspirations of most of the developing nations. Inasmuch as the relative dependence of the world on oil, as opposed to other sources of energy, is not expected to change significantly over the next decade, the importance of the Middle East to most of the nations of the globe, far from diminishing, will become increasingly binding during the 1980s.

Heightening the complexities of the region is Israel, a bone in the throat of the Arab states since its creation from the territory of Palestine in 1948. The Arab-Israeli confrontation has long been a special problem for the western powers and in more recent years has engaged the close attention of the Soviet Union. The United States, since World War II, has attempted to maintain an evenhanded policy in dealing with the Israelis and the Arabs and has sought a more lasting, if not permanent, political solution to the innumerable problems involved. But success has been elusive. Repeated rounds of hostilities have erupted followed by repeated flurries of diplomatic moves. In the meantime, both sides have acquired armaments of increasing lethality, range, and sophistication, and the successive rounds of fighting have become more intense and have engulfed a wider area. In the recent past, the hostilities have involved an increasingly grave possibility of direct confrontation between U.S. and Soviet forces.

To complicate matters further, Iran, with the help of primarily the United States, has become the dominant power in the Persian Gulf and has moved in to fill the vacuum created by the withdrawal of British forces from the area a few years ago. This naturally has exacerbated Iranian relations with Saudi Arabia, not to mention the Arab states on the southern littoral of the gulf. Iran now effectively controls the vital Strait of Hormuz, astride the oil artery which sustains the economy of Japan and is almost as important to the United States, its NATO allies, and some nonaligned countries. The rise of Iran is a double-edged sword for the United States—on the one hand, it enhances the security of the Persian Gulf (assuming that the Shah and his western-oriented regime remain in power); but on the other hand, it encourages the ambitions of this powerful, wealthy state and correspondingly reduces the politico-military influence of the United States in the region.

The Arab-Israeli conflict may soon reach a point of no return. The outbreak of fresh hostilities might precipitate a much wider war, even a global one. The area is a ticking time bomb. With Soviet influence in the Middle East degraded, the United States now finds itself once again in the unenviable position of having to support both sides in a renewed war. The anomalies of this situation are dramatic: recently, for example, the United States agreed to provide maintenance for Egyptian combat aircraft which the Soviet Union had originally supplied without adequate spare parts and logistic backup.[10]

If hostilities recur, Israel, with its definite military edge, will probably emerge the victor. The damage, direct and collateral, to both sides will probably be considerably heavier and more widespread than has occurred to date. This raises again the possibility that the Soviet Union would intervene, as it has threatened to do, and the very likely possibility that the Arabs would impose another oil embargo, posing the most severe challenges to the United States, Western Europe, and Japan. The attitude and actions of the Soviet Union in such contingencies, of course, would be critical to the plans and actions of the United States and its allies.

In terms of relative conventional military capabilities in the eastern Mediterranean and Persian Gulf areas, the United States and the Soviet Union appear to be at about a standoff. The Soviet Union is closer to the Middle East than the United States, but the United States is superior in strategic airlift and amphibious lift and in overall ability to deploy conventional forces into the area. The Soviet Union lacks a strong amphibious and naval capacity to deploy forces by sea and NATO controls the Turkish Straits, the passage leading from the Black Sea to the Mediterranean. Although the U.S. Sixth Fleet would have difficulty operating in the confined spaces of the eastern Medi-

[10] George C. Wilson, "U.S. Firms May Fix Egyptian Fighters, State Department Reveals," *Washington Post*, September 16, 1977.

terranean, especially in the face of the threat from Soviet submarines, antiship missiles, and long-range aircraft, and although the waters of the Persian Gulf are likewise restricted in space, the Soviet Union cannot match the overall power of a modern U.S. carrier task force. Both the United States and the Soviet Union can move forces into the area by air, the Soviet Union by overflying Turkey or Iran and the United States via bases in the Azores, Spain, or Germany, or direct from North America using air refueling. Overall, the advantages of experience and know-how lie with the United States. In the final analysis, however, national decisions of this nature and gravity would be made on the basis of the perceived national interest, and the U.S. interests in the Middle East are far more critical than the interests of the Soviet Union.

If disastrous situations are to be avoided, the time may be approaching for the United States to consider seriously a multilateral cooperative effort involving U.S. and Soviet participation in an international peace-keeping operation in the Middle East. It can be argued persuasively, moreover, that such an effort would be an effective form of conventional arms control since it would dampen, if not halt, the unending arms race between Israel and the Arab states.

The United States has been reluctant in the past to take part in such peace-keeping operations, whether or not sponsored by the United Nations. Shortly after World War II, the American delegation to the newly established United Nations in New York City included a military element headed by Lieutenant General Matthew B. Ridgway, U.S. Army (later to become the Eighth Army commander in Korea and the chief of staff of the U.S. Army), which was actively engaged in planning for possible American participation in peace-keeping ventures as provided for in the UN Charter. However, early in its career as a member of the United Nations, the United States adopted a policy of avoiding great power participation in peace-keeping forces, presumably because a Soviet military presence in potentially contested areas was deemed undesirable, if not unacceptable. Nevertheless, the United States fought the Korean War under UN sanction (after the Soviet delegate's flukish failure to exercise a veto in the UN Security Council in June 1950); it intervened unilaterally in Lebanon in 1958 with a peace-keeping force; it intervened in the Dominican Republic in 1965 with a peace-keeping force later supported by the Organization of American States and transformed into the Inter-American Peace Force, the first of its kind; and in 1975 it established a surveillance operation in the Sinai, manned by U.S. civilians, to monitor the passes in the UN buffer zone between Egyptian and Israeli forces occupied by the UN Emergency Force.

Other political and diplomatic moves, of course, should be exhausted first, but in the end, the United States may not have any workable alternative for the Arab-Israeli impasse than to take the initiative in imposing a political solution. The United States should not reject out of hand the option of using military force, since to foreclose the use or the credible threat of force certainly does not strengthen our negotiating position. Finally, a great power peace-keeping force may be required in the long run to maintain peace following a freely negotiated settlement. UN and other peace-keeping forces are not new to the Middle East; indeed, a Syrian-Saudi Arabian-Sudanese peace-keeping force is in Lebanon now trying to maintain a cease-fire. It may be that the great powers that allowed the creation of Israel in the first place will ultimately have to stand guard over its continued existence.

In summary, the Middle East will remain vital to U.S. interests over the next decade, and any national strategy must give priority attention to the protection of those interests.

The Pacific Basin. Although the United States historically has taken a keen interest in the Western Pacific, it was not until the Spanish-American War and the temporary acquisition of the Philippines that the United States found itself with major international responsibilities in the Far East. In the 1920s and 1930s, the rise of American naval power in the Pacific was bound to clash sooner or later with the maritime ambitions of the island empire of Japan; the explosion came at Pearl Harbor on December 7, 1941. Since then, the United States has committed its military power in the Pacific in three wars—World War II, Korea, and Vietnam. In addition, the Pacific orientation of the states of Hawaii and Alaska, which joined the Union in this period, has drawn its attention toward the East.

Immediately after World War II, U.S. strategic war planning visualized holding only the offshore island chain in the Western Pacific—the Aleutians, Japan and the Ryukus, Taiwan, and the Philippines. The two most important strategic areas in the Pacific were considered to be Northeast Asia, centering on Japan, and the Southwest Pacific, focusing on another island nation, Indonesia. As an exception to the island chain concept, it was envisioned that any hostile incursion towards Singapore would be blocked on the mainland at the Isthmus of Kra, the narrowest part of the Malayan Peninsula, where Thailand and Malaysia now come together. In this way, any land approach to Singapore and the Strait of Malacca could be denied. At the other end of the island chain, our interests at the time with respect to Korea were ambiguous and this was one of the factors leading to the Korean War. Since that conflict, the United States has made clear that it would defend the Republic of Korea.

Korea, the first limited war fought by the United States and not a completely satisfactory one, nevertheless was fought under circumstances that favored the U.S. and other UN forces. The defense of the relatively narrow ground front over which most of the war was fought was well within the ground combat means made available to the U.S.-UN forces, and U.S. forces controlled the sea flanks and the air space over the arena. Moreover, there was no serious guerrilla threat in the rear, as the enemy simply was unable to infiltrate agents or supplies by land, sea, or air to any significant degree. As a result, the North Koreans and Chinese suffered enormous casualties in fruitless, senseless frontal assaults and had nothing to show for their sacrifices when a truce was finally negotiated in July 1953.

Vietnam was quite a different story. The United States fought that war under the most severe strategic disadvantages—political, psychological, military, and sociological; and a basic understanding of the nature of the war on our part came late. A coherent overall strategy was lacking, and the strategy pursued in the ground war—a strategy of attrition—was fatally flawed. The United States was faced with defending South Vietnam from within its own borders—over 900 miles of land border, mostly heavy jungle, much of it mountainous and ill-defined, and over 1,400 miles of coastline. To seal off this vast area from infiltration was virtually impossible. Thus in a sense, the American defeat should not have been altogether surprising. Nevertheless, it can be said that in a larger context our efforts were not completely in vain. During the ten years from the time we committed our forces in strength in 1965 to the collapse of Saigon in 1975, other noncommunist nations in the area benefited greatly from our actions. Malaysia and Singapore recorded a remarkable period of political, economic, and social growth. But of even greater significance was the countercoup in September 1965 which saved Indonesia from almost certain Communist conquest. The fact that the United States had committed its power and prestige in Vietnam was without doubt a major factor in the success of the countercoup. Indonesia is the strategic prize in Southeast Asia. Occupying the world's largest archipelago, this nation of about 130 million people, vastly rich in natural resources, has the talent and potential to become one of the world's power centers. Its strategic importance is enhanced by its geographic position with respect to the Strait of Malacca, one of the major international waterways of the globe. Had Indonesia gone the other way, the threat to Australia, the Philippines, Singapore, Malaysia, and New Zealand would have become very real.

Other nations in the Western Pacific likewise prospered during the Vietnam War under our security shield. Japan, the Republic of Korea, and Taiwan have done particularly well. Had the United States not fought on the side of South Vietnam, the position of all our Pacific allies would have been seriously eroded.

The area surrounding Japan is still the most important part of the Western Pacific to the United States. Since World War II, Japan has been a steadfast, loyal, and powerful friend of the United States. Now an economic giant in its own right, Japan is destined in the 1980s to become even more important economically. Japan, however, has been shaken by our announced intention to withdraw U.S. ground combat forces from South Korea in the early 1980s and is no doubt rethinking its own security posture and reviewing its base rights commitments to the United States. These commitments are critical to the American position in the Western Pacific. Thus we must do our utmost to reassure Japan about our intention to provide for its overall defense.

The decision to withdraw U.S. troops from South Korea has had a similarly sobering effect on the South Korean government itself. Unquestionably, the security of the Republic of Korea has been weakened, for nothing can substitute for the presence on the ground of U.S. combat troops. Compensating U.S. military aid will partially offset this loss, and it is critically important that the United States not renege in this matter. In other words, the defense of South Korea must be maintained at a level sufficiently high to discourage any thought on the part of the North Koreans that on their own they can challenge the South militarily. But there is another troublesome aspect to our decision—it definitely reduces U.S. leverage and influence in the very strategic part of the world where the Soviet Union, China, and Japan meet.

Militarily, our ability to protect U.S. interests in the region during the 1980s will depend in large part on the continued availability of bases. It goes without saying that the United States must maintain its technological efficiency and must continue to modernize its forces deployed in the area. The Soviet Union faces a disadvantage in the hostile climate of Northeast Asia, and its naval forces might be bottled up in the Sea of Japan and the Sea of Okhotsk. These seas, however, so close to home, are also Soviet sanctuaries and would be penetrated only with difficulty by U.S. forces. Moreover, the Soviet submarine threat in the Pacific could be formidable. On balance, provided that the American military presence in the Western Pacific is not further reduced, the United States should be able to maintain a position of considerable influence in the region during the next decade.

The question of Taiwan will no doubt be settled some time during the next ten years. The People's Republic of China, absorbed in its own domestic reformation and growth, has no overriding interest in the United States except U.S. support in the Sino-Soviet rift. Taiwan cannot be more than a peripheral, although contentious, issue to the People's Republic. Yet for the United States, Taiwan is a painful reminder of a solemn defense commitment. Inasmuch as the People's Republic has little to offer the United States other than friendship and good will, there appear to be grossly insufficient reasons to abandon Taiwan and abrogate our defense treaty. Moreover, once Taiwan were cut loose for the sake of better Sino-American relations, we would have lost any "quid" to exchange for more concrete evidence of the sincerity of China's desire for normal relations. From a defense point of view, we must recognize that the loss of Taiwan would not only eliminate an important U.S. base in the Pacific, but also would break the strategic offshore island defense chain. Chinese missiles on Taiwan surely would increase the threat and pressure on Japan and the Philippines, and thus would further erode American influence in this central portion of the Pacific basin.

Today, American prosperity is linked to the nations of the Pacific basin. In 1975, our trade with the Far East exceeded our trade with Europe. The American economy is a major user of raw materials from the Orient and a major consumer of Asian goods, and it looks to Asian markets for export and investment opportunities. Japan is not only our most important partner in foreign trade but is also a major trading partner of the Soviet Union and China.[11]

What about tomorrow—the 1980s? According to Herman Kahn, the Pacific basin could become "an efficient connector rather than a barrier," and in the next decade the countries of the basin (including some like Brazil which do not border on the Pacific Ocean but are becoming increasingly involved with the Pacific nations) could form a "relatively tight trading and investment community." An amalgam of cultures comparable to those that arose in the Mediterranean and North Atlantic regions would be created, a mixture of Western, Chinese, and East Indian cultures. Kahn points out that the single most important factor in linking this immense basin together would be the continuation of the extraordinary economic growth it has achieved since World War II—a trend deemed likely for the future. The other ingredients he mentions, in addition to the natural attributes of the sea as a carrier and the expected technological advances in ocean-going ships, are new telecommunications systems sorely needed to tie organizations together and the further stimulus of supersonic

[11] "U.S. Defense Needs," AUSA Paper, p. 6.

aircraft to move key personnel and high-value materiel. The accomplishments of the recent past support the optimistic conclusion that Kahn's bullish remarks are justified.[12]

In summary, the United States has vital interests in Japan and Northeast Asia and important interests in the Southwest Pacific, where Indonesia may emerge someday as a new giant on the world scene. Any national strategy must take into account the present overall importance of the Pacific basin and its extraordinary potential for the next decade or two.

Africa, the Subcontinent of Asia, and the Indian Ocean. The importance of North Africa and its Mediterranean littoral, as well as the Horn of Africa, has been highlighted in the discussions of Europe and the Middle East. Let us now address briefly Africa south of the Sahara—Black Africa. This area possesses strategic importance in terms of critical natural resources, for example, manganese and chromium; and Nigeria is the second largest supplier, next to Saudi Arabia, of foreign oil to the United States.[13] Moreover, bases in southern Africa, if available to the United States and its allies, could be of great value in the event the heavy flow of oil tankers from Middle East fields to western countries around the Cape of Good Hope were threatened. The pervasive presence of Soviet military and economic aid, not to mention Cuban volunteers, is worrisome for the future.

Southern Africa is also of great political, psychological, and cultural moment to a growing and articulate segment of our population with increasing political and economic clout of its own within the American system. The very understandable and emotional interest of black Americans in Black Africa is important to our nation and must not be neglected. But it must also be constantly borne in mind that the United States has no vital interests in this region. Our current course of action—in effect, heavy-handed, overt political and economic intervention—is risky, for its failure could lead, at the very least, to our being blamed on all sides, and at most to a bloody conflagration over a vast territory which might result in direct U.S. military involvement. We must proceed with extraordinary prudence and patience, avoiding at all costs any commitment of U.S. military power in the area. Strategically, Africa is a morass, and any U.S. military

[12] Herman Kahn, "To What Extent Will the Pacific Ocean Become an Efficient Connector instead of a Barrier?" *Washington Post*, December 9, 1977.

[13] Dusko Doder, "First Visit to U.S. by Nigerian Leader Set," *Washington Post*, September 13, 1977.

engagement there would be not only more complex and difficult than half a dozen Vietnams, but also disastrous for the United States.

The United States has an important political, economic, psychological, and social interest in the future of the subcontinent of Asia, especially India, another possible world power center, though not likely to emerge as such in the foreseeable future. But again, the United States has no vital interests in the region and should be very careful to avoid any military entanglement there. Like Africa, India could become an uncontrollable quagmire.

The Indian Ocean is unique in that it contains not only the oil tanker lifelines of Japan, NATO, and the United States, but also the principal maritime route between the Soviet Far East and the western Soviet Union. Yet neither the U.S. Navy nor the Soviet navy can totally guarantee freedom of navigation along these routes. So long as hostile military actions do not threaten their respective routes, neither the United States nor the Soviet Union has truly vital interests in the region. Thus there is a basis for a mutually advantageous U.S.-Soviet agreement to limit naval deployments and naval bases in the area.[14]

Outline of an Emerging National Strategy. The foregoing assessment suggests a strategy for the 1980s of selective engagement, opposing the expansion of potentially hostile states on the Eurasian land mass into selected areas on or outside that land mass that are of vital interest to the United States, while maintaining access for those allies, friends, and neutral nations whose geopolitical positions, natural resources, or markets are of critical importance to the United States. Concurrently, the United States would engage in essentially nonmilitary competition in other parts of the world and would participate in providing economic aid for selected recipients where this appeared to be in our own interest. As a general rule, U.S. military aid would not be used for essentially political purposes, but would be predicated strictly on the nature of the threat to the United States and to the recipient, the potential military performance of the recipient, and the degree of control the United States could expect to exercise over the recipient.[15]

[14] "Controlling the Conventional Arms Race," *UN-USA National Policy Panel on Conventional Arms Control*, UN Association of the USA, New York, New York, November 1976. See also Dale R. Tahtinen, *Arms in the Indian Ocean* (Washington, D.C.: American Enterprise Institute, 1977).

[15] Robert J. Pranger and Dale R. Tahtinen, *Towards a Realistic Military Assistance Program* (Washington, D.C.: American Enterprise Institute, 1974).

Basically deterrent, this strategy seeks to avoid a general nuclear war between the United States and the Soviet Union and to limit unavoidable hostilities to conventional nonnuclear warfare. It recognizes the growing interdependence of all the nations of the world; it recognizes that the United States cannot survive alone, but is dependent on foreign sources of certain raw materials and goods; and it recognizes that the United States needs allies capable of providing their own defense.

An integral part of this strategy is a sustained U.S. commitment to the negotiated control of arms, both nuclear and conventional, to include effective national and international control of the worldwide arms trade. Arms control agreements which reduce armaments levels and avoid undue proliferation of arms without jeopardizing national survival or other vital national interests are clearly in the best interests of all nations. Negotiations over the control of conventional arms have not received as much attention as strategic arms limitation talks and deserve increased U.S. interest. In this connection, some linkage between the U.S.-Soviet SALT talks and the NATO-Warsaw Pact talks on Mutual and Balanced Force Reductions in Central Europe (MBFR) is not only inevitable but probably desirable. For example, future agreements should not restrict cruise missiles in such a way as to deny development of them by any NATO allies that want to establish their own direct nuclear deterrent to Soviet nuclear strike forces.

Implicit in this strategy is the need for the United States, with the help of its allies, to maintain technological superiority in nuclear and nonnuclear weapons systems, mobility systems, and communications systems. In particular, qualitative superiority in our strategic nuclear weapons systems is mandatory if we are to assure our survival on an assured second strike basis. As for conventional war, the American way involves a high machine-to-man ratio, superior fighting men, and massive, accurate firepower.

Energy sources for our economy and our armed forces are an essential element of any strategy. Energy shortages and costs are not expected to be a significant limiting factor in the 1980s, but beyond that date and in the early twenty-first century could become the dominant factor in our entire domestic and foreign posture, economic and military. Perhaps the most severely affected element will be transportation. While it appears that technology should solve our land transportation problems, fuel for ships poses a much greater challenge, and fuel for aircraft is easily the most severe problem of all.

A workable strategy should, of course, be reasonably attainable with our resources and must have a good chance of gaining political and public acceptance. The strategy advocated in this chapter meets these criteria. Let us next take a closer look at the military component of the strategy.

Defense Planning

From this strategy and the foregoing assessment, there naturally flows a set of defense priorities in the event of general hostilities which in turn form the basis for U.S. defense programs. These priorities are:

(1) Defense of the United States, in cooperation with Canada, against aerospace attack

- Internal security of the United States
- Defense of lines of communication (LOCs), primarily sea and air, from the United States to critical parts of the Western Hemisphere, in particular the Caribbean region but including the Panama Canal, Canada, Brazil, and Mexico

(2) Defense of NATO

- Defense of sea and air LOCs to the oil fields of the Middle East assuring access to Middle East oil for the United States, Western Europe, and Japan

(3) Defense of sea and air LOCs from the United States to Western Europe through the North Atlantic, and from the United States to Northeast Asia through the Pacific

(4) Defense of Northeast Asia

(5) Defense of sea and air LOCs from the United States to the Southwest Pacific (the Philippines, Indonesia, Singapore, Malaysia, Australia, and New Zealand)

In addition to general war priority tasks there are, of course, numerous likely confrontation situations short of general war which might require the employment of U.S. forces. These include disorders in Panama, another Arab-Israeli war, and participation in peacekeeping forces in the Middle East.

In addition to such general priorities, defense planners require considerably more detailed strategic guidance before developing specific U.S. force structures and concrete defense programs. One device used is to outline scenarios for various unfolding situations as the basis for specific force development and operational and logistic planning. For example, one scenario might assume a major war starting in Europe, while another might postulate one starting in Northeast Asia and then spreading to Europe. Another might assume a war at sea between the United States and the Soviet Union which does not escalate into a general world war, while still another might assume a local confrontation in the Middle East which expands into hostilities involving the United States. Thus, various situations are postulated with the objective of producing a sound basis for an adequate defense establishment and realistic defense planning.

The most complex, difficult, and uncertain task of defense planning is to determine specific levels for various types of forces and weapons systems for each service. On the one hand, strategic nuclear force planning can be readily quantified since only the United States and the Soviet Union need to be considered (at least at this time) and the relative capabilities of each side's nuclear arsenal can be accurately computed. Determining the appropriate size for conventional forces, on the other hand, is not a matter of trying to offset total Soviet capabilities in every category. Instead, it is a matter of analyzing U.S. force requirements (in addition to possible allied contributions) only in those operational arenas where vital U.S. interests are involved. Conventional warfare, moreover, is far more complex than nuclear warfare, involving a multitude of different types of military units and weapons, U.S. and allied, and many unquantifiable yet most significant intangibles such as leadership, training, morale, terrain, and weather.

For the United States, NATO's needs are relatively easy to quantify since the arena and the contenders are known in advance. The NATO theater generates the largest and most demanding U.S. force requirement, particularly for the U.S. Army and the tactical elements of the U.S. Air Force, and, therefore, determines the conventional force structures of these two services.

Let us turn now to a more detailed analysis of our defenses—specifically, of the significant choices facing defense planners in the following areas:

- strategic nuclear forces,
- general purpose forces (conventional land, sea, and air),
- strategic mobility forces (that is, long-range air and sealift),
- operational bases at home and overseas,
- support forces (military and civilian),
- technological and industrial base, and
- mobilization capacity.

Without attempting to be comprehensive, this discussion will emphasize those aspects that are critical to the suggested strategy.

Strategic Nuclear Forces. The prospects are that the United States will have no choice but to give the highest priority to nuclear weapons technology in order to safeguard U.S. options to cope with developments which might disturb any nuclear balance sanctioned by SALT. Although our present relative posture does not appear to call for any crash programs, prudent planning should include the continuous exploration of advanced antiballistic missile (ABM) technology, advanced antisubmarine warfare (ASW) technology, especially against ballistic missile submarines, and civil defense alternatives, as well as various possible qualitative improvements of our offensive systems.

With respect to the components of the offensive Triad (strategic bombers, land-based intercontinental ballistic missiles and submarine-launched ballistic missiles), the long-term implications of the decision to cancel production of the B-1 strategic bomber are disturbing. Some have interpreted the decision to mean the eventual demise of the bomber component and of the whole Triad concept as known today. To allow this to happen would be a serious mistake. In addition to the obvious advantage of adding to the magnitude and complexity of the problems facing the Soviet defense planner, the strategic bomber exploits a technology in which the United States has long held a substantial lead. To give up this advantage with no compensating concession from the Soviet Union makes no sense. But perhaps the most important advantage of the bomber is its unequalled usefulness in a crisis. In a nuclear showdown, placing nuclear-armed SAC bombers on higher states of alert, ground and airborne, and dispersing and deploying them away from home bases would create a more visible American signature than any other action based on the Triad. Moreover, nuclear ready bombers can be launched towards their targets and yet still be recalled with safety: this is a unique capability of great value. One has to conclude that the bomber remains an indispensable leg of the Triad.

General Purpose Forces. Whereas at one time the United States could meet Soviet threats by simply increasing the alert and readiness status of its strategic nuclear forces, today and increasingly in the future, the United States must rely on its general-purpose conventional forces at times of international tension. For example, in the Arab-Israeli fighting in October 1973, when the Soviet Union alerted its airborne divisions as an obvious threat of intervention on the side of Egypt, the United States responded not only by readying SAC but also by deploying a full range of conventional forces. The moves of the Sixth

Fleet in the eastern Mediterranean, the alerting of the 82nd Airborne Division and U.S. Air Force tactical air units in the continental United States, the airlift and subsequent sealift to Israel of tanks, tank ammunition, and other urgently needed items, and the nonstop, air-refueled delivery of U.S. Air Force F-4s to Tel Aviv—all of these actions together were no doubt convincing to the Soviet Union.

Handling local conflicts and participating in peace-keeping undertakings, as important as they may be, however, involve lower stakes than the need to deter Soviet and Warsaw Pact forces in Europe. Here the manpower restraints of the peacetime all-volunteer force concept, the lack of a standby selective service system, and the lack of a fully credible mobilization capability are bothersome weaknesses in our conventional force posture, particularly if the Soviet Union continues to improve its conventional forces in position in Eastern Europe.

Every component of Soviet conventional forces—land, sea, and air—is being qualitatively improved. Powerful, accurate, sophisticated military gear—including armor, artillery, mechanized infantry, air defense weapons, helicopters, tactical fighters and reconnaissance aircraft, and naval combatants, surface and subsurface—is being produced in quantity. Again, the United States must retain some degree of technological superiority, modernizing its equipment as successful new developments emerge. This is an expensive proposition, but quality forces do not come cheap.

Land forces. The present army force structure, active and reserve, should suffice for the forseeable future provided that needed modernization is achieved. (U.S. Marine Corps forces, since they are part of the Department of the Navy and normally operate with naval amphibious forces, will be discussed with the U.S. Navy.) The Army National Guard and Army Reserve are very important elements but suffer from major personnel shortfalls under the all-volunteer force. There are also major overall army equipment shortages which under present programs will take many years to correct. Adequate organic air defense weapons for units in the field, for example, are lacking. Although the army is a manpower-intensive service because of the nature of its mission, it, too, must have modern, sophisticated arms and equipment to be effective, and nothing is cheap anymore.

One ever present dilemma facing the U.S. Army (and the conventional forces of the other services) is how to shape its force structure for the kinds of warfare and theaters of war that are expected. Paradoxically, the most violent, sophisticated, and complex warfare would be expected in Europe, yet if our strategy of deterrence works, this is the least likely war to be fought. On the other hand, the army needs lighter divisions and other types of formations and weapons systems for possible use in other parts of the world. Peace-keeping and stability operations pose still another requirement. To improve the strategic air mobility of army forces means acquiring lighter, smaller units, thus further adding to the dimensions of the problem. Pre-positioning heavy equipment in a theater (Germany for example) for the heavy divisions and units earmarked for NATO is not the total answer because it is expensive in personnel and maintenance costs and wasteful of valuable equipment needed for training. Although armor, mechanized infantry, and other mechanized forces must play the dominant role in a theater such as Europe, lighter formations, such as the air mobile division (air assault division with a large number of helicopters), also have a valuable role in such intensive warfare and have great versatility for other arenas and missions. Thus, the army must make force structure and equipment decisions which are compromises and hedges in the uncertain business of war planning.

Although the U.S. Army has outstanding tactical mobility, both of ground vehicles and helicopters, and can span the largest rivers with its bridging capability, it lacks strategic mobility of its own. It is a strategic hitchhiker, dependent on the U.S. Air Force and the U.S. Navy when it must move overseas. Strategic mobility and overseas bases are critical elements of the suggested strategy and will be addressed later.

History has repeatedly shown that air and sea power cannot substitute for land power when a nation's vital interests are on the line. Air and sea power are, of course, indispensable and make the projection of land power overseas possible in the first place; they can also help support the forces of allied nations. But only land forces on the ground at the scene of conflict can decisively influence the outcome. The presence of air power or a naval task force in a potential trouble spot can be helpful in tilting a crisis situation towards a favorable outcome, but only land forces, with the necessary air and naval support, can stabilize a conflict situation on the ground and keep the peace. This is why peace-keeping forces must be essentially ground forces. However, it should be borne in mind that the presence of U.S. ground forces commits U.S. power and therefore should be deployed only in arenas that are of vital concern to the United States.

Naval and marine forces. After years of intensive operations which devoured available defense funds and postponed the modernization of an aging fleet, the U.S. Navy is finally adding modern new ships to its inventory. The pace is still slow because of the time and great cost involved, and it is doubtful whether the navy will build up its fleet to 500 active ships (from the present 470) over the next decade.[16]

With the emergence of Soviet naval power, the U.S. Navy faces two extremely complex and different questions: What kind of a navy should the United States be shaping for the future? And what kinds of ships should the navy be building? It is already very late because of the long lead time (approximately eight years) for the construction of combatant ships. Whatever new ships we decide to build in 1977 will not be launched until the late 1980s.

In recent years, the Soviet navy has made dramatic improvements and has become a major global sea power. Its strategic ballistic missile submarines can threaten the United States and its allies from any of the world's oceans. Long-range nuclear powered submarines have replaced many conventionally powered attack submarines. Modern antiship missile-equipped surface combatants and long-range naval aircraft with sophisticated electronics have been introduced. The large Soviet merchant and fishing fleets are linked to the naval forces, for which they form an effective logistic and intelligence arm. But by far the most formidable and serious threat is the enormous undersea Soviet fleet.[17]

To grasp just how formidable this threat is, let us briefly examine our experience in World War II. Before the entry of the United States, the Western Allies almost lost the war at sea in the North Atlantic to the German submarine fleet. After Pearl Harbor, before the United States could move significant ground and air forces overseas, the Allies still had a grim time getting ships safely through the North Atlantic, and the United States had an additional problem in the Caribbean and South Atlantic where German submarines were sinking our tankers faster than we could build new ones. The war hung in the balance until our combined naval forces, with some important help from the land-based aircraft of the army air forces, prevailed against the submarines. At the start of World War II, the German navy had only about 40 ocean-going attack submarines in service and by February 1941, nine months before Pearl Harbor, that number was down to 21. Compare this with today's Soviet navy, which has roughly 250 attack submarines (81 nuclear powered and the rest diesel) and 77 strategic ballistic missile submarines (58 nuclear powered). Roughly 150 of the 250 attack submarines are deployed in the Soviet northern fleet, which is available for employment in the North Atlantic. More-

[16] Norman Polmar, "The Future of Sea-Based Air," a paper presented at the Conference on Problems of Sea Power, sponsored by the American Enterprise Institute, Washington, D.C., October 6–7, 1977.

[17] Admiral Kidd, "NATO Strategic Mobility," p. II–C–8.

over, the Soviet navy has its own naval air arm, including medium-range Badger and long-range Bear aircraft, where the German navy had none. Finally, in World War II, the Allied High Command had broken the German codes, an advantage we cannot expect to enjoy against the Soviet Union.[18]

The stark reality of these numbers of Soviet submarines, far more capable than the relatively primitive German subs of World War II, points up the dimensions of the technical and doctrinal challenge facing the U.S. Navy. The traditional tactics and techniques of anti-submarine warfare are obsolete, and ASW assets currently available are grossly inadequate for the job. The navy recognizes this situation and is conducting far-ranging research and development in new ASW technology. This effort deserves urgent attention and the highest research and development priority.[19]

Much of the current controversy swirling about the U.S. Navy seems to concern its mission. "Sea control" and "projection of power" have their respective champions, each side proclaiming that one particular mission is supreme and therefore should dominate naval doctrine and determine the design of ships. In the final analysis, these arguments are pointless. Title 10, U.S. Code, prescribes the mission of the U.S. Navy, to be prepared "to conduct prompt and sustained combat operations at sea." How this mission will be carried out in actual hostilities is not completely predictable. U.S. naval capabilities must be able to handle projected enemy capabilities, in this instance the Soviet navy and a much lesser but growing naval threat from Third World nations. Other than the ballistic missile submarines of the U.S. Navy, which are dedicated to a strategic nuclear strike task, U.S. combatant ships are general-purpose or multipurpose ships, capable of performing a wide variety of naval tasks. Exactly how these multipurpose forces are employed in time of war depends on not only the nature of the war, but more significantly, how the enemy decides to employ its naval forces.

One respected school of thought, for example, argues that in the Soviet view the primary mission of the navy is a strategic one—the operation of the ballistic missile submarine fleet, the protection of this underwater nuclear strike force, and the strategic defense of the homeland against U.S. strategic nuclear forces. Under this concept,

[18] Norman Polmar, "The Threats to U.S. Sea LOC's," proceedings of the 1977 Worldwide Strategic Mobility Conference, May 2, 1977, part 2.

[19] Vice Admiral William Crowe, "Western Strategy and Naval Missions Approaching the 32nd Century," a paper presented at the Conference on Problems of Sea Power, American Enterprise Institute, October 6–7, 1977.

Soviet attack submarines would be employed principally against U.S. ballistic missile submarines threatening the motherland and against carrier task forces and any other naval forces with an ASW capability; and attacking U.S. sea lines of communication would have low priority.[20] This concept may be correct, but the United States cannot afford to base its defense plans entirely on what Soviet intentions might be; rather, it must base them on Soviet capabilities, and the Soviet submarine capability against our sea lanes is too great to ignore.

Again it can be argued that NATO ports and airfields would be so damaged once war had begun that ships could not unload and aircraft could not land, and that, therefore, the defense of sea and air lines of communication would become irrelevant anyway. This is not a sound thesis—there are other ways to unload a ship besides over a dock, and damage to port and airbase facilities can be overcome by determination and ingenuity. Great damage and destruction are the handmaidens of war, but it is the human mind and human will that have the greatest bearing on the outcome.

Another controversy centers on the future of the large aircraft carrier. It is true that the carrier is vulnerable, and increasingly so, to modern, highly accurate missiles, but so are all the other instruments of war—land, sea, and air. The constant see-saw competition between offensive and defensive weapons has been going on for centuries and will never end.

The big carrier is probably obsolescent, but it is still far from obsolete, and today it is the most formidable warship afloat. It is also true that the carrier no longer has a significant strategic nuclear role; its future role is largely a political-military one in peacetime. But it continues to have a powerful and versatile role in limited conflicts. (Incidentally, we should not repeat the mistake we made in Southeast Asia and wear out these valuable vessels in prolonged land and air campaigns for which land-based aircraft are better suited.) Since the current fleet of carriers should remain effective well through the 1980s and sea-based tactical aviation will be important to future American use of the high seas, the question becomes what kind of aircraft carriers the United States should build. Cost has become almost the dominant factor in shipbuilding decisions, and there are economy of scale advantages to building the large carrier. Nevertheless, the logical decision is to build smaller carriers and to focus on vertical and short takeoff and landing (VSTOL) aircraft technology which could greatly

[20] James M. McConnell, "Soviet Strategy and Missions," a paper presented at the Conference on Problems of Sea Power, American Enterprise Institute, October 6–7, 1977.

expand the number of ships in the fleet that could be used as platforms for versatile multipurpose aircraft.[21]

The U.S. Marine Corps, as an integral part of the Department of the Navy, is organized basically to fight as part of the navy. The Marine Division-Air Wing is a close-knit, completely integrated fighting team, designed and trained as a sea-based force, an organic component of naval amphibious forces, to be inserted ashore, whether across the beach or by air, as part of a naval campaign. The Marines are not designed, equipped, or intended to be committed in sustained combat in a land war and should not be so employed except when it is clear that the land-air battle is being lost. There may also be short-duration missions of great tactical value in the land-air battle which are suitable for the Marines. In sum, sustained land-air warfare is the business of land-based forces; sea-based forces used in this role can be worn out at an alarming rate, unacceptably compromising their ability to fulfill their primary role.

The current force structure of the Marine Corps appears to be adequate for the foreseeable future, and the forces themselves, with some minor exceptions, appear to be suitably armed and equipped for the missions envisioned. The question of how much Marine Corps air power is necessary and of what types of aircraft are suitable for what missions is one which the Marine Corps itself must solve, since a choice may have to be made between the high material costs and quality manpower demands of the Marine air arm and the requirements of the fundamental ground arm.

Tactical air forces (USAF). This discussion is limited to the United States Air Force (USAF), although the other services all possess organic tactical air elements which operate and fight in a highly integrated manner with their surface elements.

The present active USAF tactical air force structure appears to be adequate at this time provided that it is kept modern and maintained in a high state of readiness. USAF Air National Guard and Air Reserve units possess first-line types of aircraft ready for use and have achieved a state of readiness unequalled in the reserve components of any other service. Their reserve air units give the active air force a ready capability to meet sudden peak operational demands. The tactical air elements of the active forces, however, are designed for sustained operations of indefinite duration, a capability lacking in the reserve components of the USAF.

From the perspective of the crucial land battle, air superiority remains the number one mission for tactical air forces, as the lack of

---

[21] Polmar, "The Future of Sea-Based Air."

air superiority is very inhibiting to ground mobility and can stymie ground operations. Close air support, on the other hand, although always welcome, is of lower priority in the eyes of the army in view of its own organic fire support, both ground and air delivered. Air interdiction of enemy lines of communication leading to the battlefield, so long as it is conducted in coordination with the land battle, is a highly important mission from the point of view of the land battle commander. In short, the land battle is in actuality the land-air battle, and although ground and air operations are fought by separate commanders, ultimate success depends on their close coordination by the overall theater commander.

Strategic Mobility. By now it should be apparent that to support the central military thrust of the strategy suggested here requires an ability to deploy U.S. forces from the United States and to move forces, materiel, and supplies already positioned overseas. Strategic mobility is one prerequisite; the other is the availability of operational bases outside the United States. These bases are needed not only to support air and naval forces operating in the area, but also to extend the range of strategic air and sealift for the transport of troops, their equipment, and supplies.

Strategic mobility basically requires the ability to move military personnel, equipment, and supplies over long distances by air and by sea. In addition, strategic mobility requires the ability to move military forces and materiel expeditiously overland, by highways and railroad, in particular within the United States.

Air and sea transport are each important, with unique but complementary capabilities. Whereas entire units and their equipment can be moved by air if necessary, moving heavy items and bulk tonnage in large quantities by air is expensive, especially with regard to fuel. Sea transport is indispensable not only for moving forces in a reinforcing role, but also for resupplying forces, a critical mission. In fact, over the long term, 90 to 95 percent of overall military requirements must be handled by sea. The art of strategic military movement lies, therefore, in the optimum combination of air and sea transport for any given operation.

U.S. strategic airlift, in terms of assets, capabilities, know-how, and experience, has no peer. The present all-jet force of the Military Airlift Command (MAC), with less than half as many aircraft as its reciprocal-engine predecessor in the late 1960s, can move far more total tonnage in much less time and can lift single loads three times as heavy. The C-5 aircraft, although limited in numbers and composing only one-fourth of MAC's jet fleet, represents 50 percent of

MAC's strategic airlift capability; it is the only aircraft capable of carrying all the army's heavy combat vehicles. In time of emergency, MAC can be augmented by a large fleet of modern jet cargo and passenger aircraft from the designated Civil Reserve Air Fleet (CRAF). Tactical airlift aircraft assigned to MAC, which can also be used to move troops and cargo over strategic distances, are likewise unexcelled in the world but in the absence of modernization are beginning to show clear signs of age.[22]

Turbine-engined aircraft, which revolutionized airlift, commercial and military, caused a quantum jump in the number of ton-miles moved by air in the early 1970s, but their use is leveling off in the late 1970s. No comparable breakthroughs in aircraft technology are in prospect, but a steady growth of ton-miles lifted, civilian and military, of about 7 percent per year is anticipated in the 1980s as the demand for the airlift of people and high-value items expands despite the increasing cost of fuel.[23]

However, the air fleet available for a task like ferrying army troops and equipment to Europe in a reasonable time during an emergency has serious limitations. While it could carry the troops without any problem, it would not include enough wide-bodied C-5 type aircraft to carry the most bulky equipment of the army. The smaller C-141, which makes up 75 percent of MAC's fleet, lacks this outsize cargo capacity and does not have an in-flight refueling capability, which further limits its uses. We must probably make the most of the C-5, although its wing structure is faulty and will require a very costly modification to extend its useful service life. Equally expensive are the programs we need to improve our refueling capability, produce a "stretched" C-141 with a refueling capability, and modify a number of wide-bodied passenger aircraft in the CRAF enabling them to carry cargo.[24]

The U.S. capacity to transport men and materiel by sea is not so favorable. The U.S. merchant fleet has been in a steady decline since World War II, and the Military Sealift Command (MSC) has only limited assets. American-owned ships flying foreign flags are a dubious resource and other foreign-flag ships, although in service in ample numbers, cannot be relied upon in all emergencies. More U.S. cargo is now being carried on Soviet ships than on American ones. Recently, Kuwait passed new laws requiring that 40 to 60 percent of

[22] Collins, "American and Soviet Armed Services," p. S14092.

[23] General William G. Moore, Commander, U.S. Military Airlift Command, Briefing at MAC headquarters, Scott Air Force Base, Illinois, August 5, 1977.

[24] Ibid.

the oil exported from Kuwait move by Arab tankers. This action portends even greater oil crises in the future.[25]

There is a shortage of ships, as there is of aircraft, that can handle outsize army equipment and of special cargo ships that can readily handle military items like ammunition. Thus, there are sealift deficiencies which under present programs will probably not be corrected in the 1980s.[26]

As for amphibious vessels, the U.S. Navy has fewer today than it had in the late 1960s. Today, the navy can handle Marine battalion and regimental landing teams and their associated Marine air elements, but to lift a Marine Division-Air Wing team simultaneously would require most of the navy's worldwide resources, now deployed in numerous small clusters from the China Sea to the Mediterranean. Nevertheless, U.S. amphibious lift far exceeds the limited Soviet capacity. Soviet marines, known as naval infantry, number only 12,000, organized into five small separate regiments.[27]

With respect to strategic mobility overland, U.S. deficiencies needing correction include inadequate loading capacity at many bases in the continental United States and an insufficient number of rail flat cars capable of handling modern main battle tanks.[28]

Operational bases overseas. Let us now examine very briefly our situation with respect to bases overseas available to American armed forces.

On the Atlantic side of the United States, NATO bases in the United Kingdom and Europe are, of course, essential to the operations of American forces within the alliance. Only those NATO bases critical to our strategic mobility will be discussed in this paper.

(1) *Naval Bases.* In the Caribbean, Guantanamo is the key base, one of the best natural harbors in the Western Hemisphere. Roosevelt Roads in Puerto Rico is useful, but it is not an alternative to Guantanamo; it would take a very large expenditure of funds to make it anywhere near as valuable as Guantanamo.

- In the North Atlantic, bases in Iceland are essential to U.S. monitoring of the Soviet Union, and bases in the Azores would be critical to ASW operations.

---

[25] Senator Daniel K. Inouye, remarks concerning the U.S. Merchant Marine, at Conference on Problems of Sea Power, American Enterprise Institute, October 6, 1977.

[26] Collins, "American and Soviet Armed Forces," pp. S14092–93.

[27] Ibid., p. S14093.

[28] Robert S. Hamilton, Surface Seminar Report, proceedings of the 1977 Worldwide Strategic Mobility Conference, May 2, 1977.

- In the Mediterranean, Rota in Spain and Souda Bay on the island of Crete (Greece) are particularly valuable, as are Naples in Italy and Sigmella on Sicily (Italy).
- In the Pacific area, bases in Japan and South Korea are obviously important to U.S. forces defending the region, but their availability might be limited for other purposes. In Japan, the most important base is Yokosuka, but Misawa naval air base is critical for monitoring of Soviet activities as well as for ASW purposes; and Sasebo and Iwakuni (Marine air base) are also useful. The most important U.S. base in the Western Pacific, however, is Subic Bay in the Philippines, considered essential for the forward operations of the Seventh Fleet. Here it should be borne in mind that Japan's energy lifeline through this area is protected by the presence of the Seventh Fleet. There is no alternative to Subic Bay for the U.S. Navy; without this indispensable base, the capabilities of the Seventh Fleet would be severely reduced.
- In the Indian Ocean, a base on Diego Garcia would no doubt be invaluable in maintaining a U.S. naval presence in that region. But as has already been pointed out, an alternative course of action would be to seek an agreement with the Soviet Union to demilitarize the area.

(2) *Air Bases.* In the Atlantic area, the most important bases for strategic mobility purposes, other than those in Canada, are Lajes air base in the Azores, Torrejon in Spain, and Rhein-Main in West Germany. These are critical to airlift operations into the Mediterranean area and the Middle East. Using in-flight refueling techniques, airlift operations from these bases could be extended into about two-thirds of Africa south of the Sahara, as well as much of the South Atlantic and the eastern Indian Ocean.

- For airlift operations in the Western Pacific, Yakota in Japan, Kadena air base on Okinawa (Japan), and Clarke air base in the Philippines are critical. Air refueling could extend operations from these bases into Singapore and other parts of the Southwest Pacific area. Anderson air base on Guam is not far enough west to be useful. Clarke air base is the largest U.S. military installation outside of the United States; its loss not only would degrade airlift capabilities into the Southwest Pacific, but also would deprive the United States of a very useful base for air operations in support of the Seventh Fleet.

The foregoing discussion suggests that attention should continue to be devoted to retaining U.S. rights to these most important overseas bases.

Technological and industrial base. The U.S. technological base remains unsurpassed and is capable of doing almost anything American leaders ask of it. There are areas where the United States is clearly ahead and others where the Soviet Union is clearly superior, but the United States can nevertheless compete in any area and produce superior results whenever policies and priorities are supportive. However, the fact remains that U.S. predominance in research and development shows some signs of weakening.

The U.S. industrial base is no longer the "Arsenal of Democracy," as it was in World War II. Industrial facilities capable of manufacturing heavy military gear, main battle tanks, for example, are less numerous than in the past, and many items formerly produced in the United States are now either partially or completely manufactured outside the country. Steps are being taken to improve the military production base (for example, the manufacture of explosives) but gaps remain. Industrial mobilization planning, in the form of close and continuous liaison between civilian and military officials, is no longer mantained.

Mobilization capacity. Our ability to mobilize has already been touched upon several times, in terms of both industrial and manpower mobilization planning or the lack thereof. The importance of this capacity as part of our overall deterrent strategy and philosophy has also been stressed.

The reserve components of our armed forces, especially those of the army, play a vital role in our overall defense posture. Some reserve elements have been criticized for a lack of readiness and poor training, but it should be borne in mind that they are important regardless of their posture. First, they are a constant reminder among our populace of the need for national defense. Active forces tend to be clustered around major bases on our coasts and within our southern tier of states, whereas National Guard and reserve units are found in all fifty states of the Union. Their presence, especially in states with few or no active forces stationed within their borders, is psychologically important, aside from the fact that they are available for duty in the event of natural disasters or civil disorders. Second, reserve components are an essential part of the U.S. mobilization capacity which in turn is an integral part of our overall deterrent posture. Herman Kahn has expounded a "mobilization warfare" thesis that makes much sense and credits the U.S. partial mobilization at the time of the Korean War with probably having deterred World War III.[29]

Forward deployments in the NATO area and in the Western Pacific, combined with air and naval bases which allow the United States to exploit the strategic mobility of its forces, are fundamental to the suggested strategy of selective engagement. This posture allows us to defend our interests in those areas considered vital to our well-being and survival; to foster our interests and help friends in the Third World; to promote international trade; and to maintain the American economy, the linchpin of the economy not just of the West but of the world.

Summary

The suggested strategy for the 1980s is believed both to be feasible—that is, supportable in the context of a national consensus that vital U.S. interests are directly threatened—and to have a reasonable chance of achievement in an economic and military sense. Everything depends on the human element—on what the people think. In my opinion, the American people are still vital and strong. They remain quite equal to the task of rising to the occasion when their survival is threatened and their aspirations are challenged.

[29] Herman Kahn, *The Technological Requirements of Mobilization Warfare* (Croton-on-the-Hudson, N.Y.: The Hudson Institute, 1976).

CONTRIBUTORS

GENERAL BRUCE K. HOLLOWAY, U.S. Air Force—Retired, commanded U.S. Air Forces, Europe and the Fourth Allied Tactical Air Force in Germany from 1965 to 1966; served as the Vice Chief of Staff, U.S. Air Force, from 1966 to 1968; and commanded the Strategic Air Command from 1968 until his retirement in 1972.

GENERAL THEODORE R. MILTON, U.S. Air Force—Retired, commanded the Thirteenth Air Force from 1961 to 1962; served as Chief of Staff, Tactical Air Command from 1965 to 1967, as the Inspector General, U.S. Air Force from 1967 to 1969, and as the U.S. Representative to the NATO Military Committee from 1969 until his retirement in 1974.

GENERAL BRUCE PALMER, JR., U.S. Army—Retired, commanded U.S. forces in the Dominican Republic, 1965 to 1966, concurrently serving as the Deputy Commander of the Inter-American Peace Force; commanded XVIII Airborne Corps from 1966 to 1967 and II Field Force, Vietnam in 1967; served as Deputy Commander, U.S. Army, Vietnam from 1967 to 1968 and as the Vice Chief of Staff, U.S. Army from 1968 to 1973; and commanded the U.S. Readiness Command from 1973 until his retirement in 1974.

GENERAL MAXWELL D. TAYLOR served as Chief of Staff, U.S. Army from 1955 until his retirement in 1959; recalled to active duty by President Kennedy and served as Chairman of the Joint Chiefs of Staff from 1962 to 1964, as Ambassador to the Republic of Vietnam from 1964 to 1965, and as Special Consultant to President Johnson from 1965 to 1969; served as President of the Institute for Defense Analyses from 1966 to 1969 and President of the Foreign Intelligence Advisory Board from 1965 to 1970.

ADMIRAL ELMO R. ZUMWALT, JR., U.S. Navy—Retired, commanded U.S. naval forces in Vietnam from 1968 to 1970 and served as the Chief of Naval Operations, U.S. Navy, from 1970 until his retirement in 1974.